"*Your Next Leap of Faith* is a compelling book that challenges readers to step out in faith and follow God's voice, regardless of the cost. With biblical wisdom and personal stories, this book will encourage you to embrace the wild ride of this life of faith. It's a must-read for anyone seeking to grow in their relationship with God and boldly pursue their calling."

Mike Signorelli, lead pastor, V1 Church

"In a time of complacent, cultural, and comfortable Christianity, Shane stands tall as a man of God. His boldness is refreshing. Shane is not a man who learned passively; he learned by standing strong, from the sands of the Middle East as a soldier to the mean streets as a police officer. He is a man of God's Word and an example to all of what a son of God should look like."

Ken Harrison, chairman, Promise Keepers

"Shane's testimony of the work of Christ and the power of the Gospel is a true source of inspiration and encouragement to us all. He challenges and provokes anyone satisfied with ordinary to trust in Christ and to be on mission for the extraordinary."

Ryan Helfenbein, executive director, Standing for Freedom Center; senior vice president of communications and public engagement, Liberty University

your next leap of faith

how to hear God's voice and boldly follow

SHANE WINNINGS

Chosen

a division of Baker Publishing Group
Minneapolis, Minnesota

© 2023 by Shane Winnings

Published by Chosen Books
Minneapolis, Minnesota
www.chosenbooks.com

Chosen Books is a division of
Baker Publishing Group, Grand Rapids, Michigan

Printed in the United States of America

ISBN 978-0-8007-6341-1 (trade paper)
ISBN 978-1-4934-4228-7 (ebook)
ISBN 978-0-8007-6360-2 (casebound)
Library of Congress Cataloging-in-Publication Control Number: 2023011579

Scripture quotations are from the New King James Version®. Copyright © 1982 by Thomas Nelson. Used by permission. All rights reserved.

The contents of this book should not be construed as medical advice.

All photos by Shane Winnings.

Baker Publishing Group publications use paper produced from sustainable forestry practices and post-consumer waste whenever possible.

23 24 25 26 27 28 29   7 6 5 4 3 2 1

To my Lord and Savior, Jesus Christ, without whom my life would be meaningless and void.

To my wife, Jessica. Thank you for loving me and supporting me so well. Thank you for being a woman of faith and integrity. It has been an honor to stand by your side and walk through life together. Here's to decades and decades more to come.

To my son, Elijah. I love you, buddy, and I can't wait for you to grow up and hear all the things God has done for our family. You are a miracle and a testimony of His faithfulness.

To my new baby who's in mommy's tummy as I write this, I can't wait to meet you and see who you'll become. May God do in you more abundantly than what He's done in me. I love you.

Contents

1

Being Willing to Face the Truth

I grew up in church for twenty-five years: volunteering, attending youth services and camps, and even spending seven years on the worship team at a megachurch. By the time I was eleven years old, I was a two-time state champion for Bible memorization with the AWANA program. I had been baptized, professed my faith publicly, and even stood up to atheists making fun of Jesus on social media. All my friends were from church. I sometimes listened to worship music in the car, played a sermon from a favorite speaker, or even listened to Christian podcasts. Most of my friends knew that I was a Christian, as I didn't hide it. When I remembered, I even prayed before most of my meals and prayed before bed each night. Even with all this, on January 23, 2016, God said the following words that cut me to the core and changed my life forever.

"Shane, you've never lived for me one day in your life."

God

How does one get to this point? How does someone who's spent a quarter of a century in the house of God receive a rebuke like this? Is it possible to spend your whole life within the walls of a church but have never actually *lived* for God? When faced with this kind of confrontation from the Almighty, you are forced to take one of two routes.

First, you can challenge God, justify your life based on your human wisdom and ability, and insist that He is wrong. You can pull out your Christian résumé and begin to argue each point, like a defense lawyer in a courtroom attempting to undermine the prosecution's case. Point by point, you can remind God of the years of faithfulness and service you have provided to Him and His house (the church). You can vehemently request that He check again because, from your view, based on your knowledge and wisdom, He must have missed something.

Second, despite this interruption, you can examine your life through this new perspective and try to see how it is possible that God is right and that you are wrong. Given this newfound ability to see your life in retrospect based on God's opinion, you can humble yourself, confess your wrong, and make a conscious effort to turn away from that life and walk into the new one God is calling you to. You can let the Bible take authority over your life and submit to the verse, "Let God be true but every man a liar" (Romans 3:4).

Let me elaborate. In 2021, I read Matthew 7, where Jesus talks about the narrow path and the wide road of destruction. Jesus is explaining that many are on the wide road, and few will find the narrow path that leads through the narrow gate of life. He then goes on to say,

> "Not everyone who says to Me, 'Lord, Lord,' shall enter the kingdom of heaven, but he who does the will of My Father in heaven. Many will say to Me in that day, 'Lord, Lord, have we not prophesied in Your name, cast out demons in Your name, and done many wonders in Your name?' And then I will declare to them, 'I never knew you; depart from Me, you who practice lawlessness!'"
>
> Matthew 7:21–23

When I read this, I saw something I'd never seen before. In verse 22, the people are presenting a rebuttal to the Lord. A rebuttal, of all things! Imagine standing before the Lord, perfect and all-knowing, sitting on His throne, and challenging His decision. I had read this passage many times, but this time in particular, verse 22, hit home to me. They respond to his decision with "didn't we do this and this and this in your name?"

By this time, the Lord has already given His verdict, and these people have been found guilty. The interaction picks up in verse 22, where we see their response to His decision, and clearly, they do not agree. That is the first problem: a lack of humility. Again, let God be true, and every man a liar. The reality is that on that day, nothing said in the presence of God will hold more weight than what He has spoken.

Now, why am I getting into all this? It seems kind of heavy, especially for the opening chapter of a book about faith. The reality is, the weight of this moment, this eternal perspective of standing before the Lord, hit me in January 2016. When God spoke to me and said that I'd never lived for Him one day of my entire life, I felt as if I were already standing before Him on Judgment Day, His verdict given.

I was powerless. I was small. I was not proud and ready to boast in my Christian résumé. I was humbled and repentant to the point of desperate weeping. I was instantly aware of my sin, my guilt before the Lord, and how my life had become all about me—my wants, desires, and needs—and how I'd simply used God as a servant whom I would reach out to when I needed something done. Oh, the agony! I could barely take the pain. But then, His love rushed in, and I felt something I'd never felt before. A peace flooded over me, and a knowing that I was forgiven consumed my being. I vowed in that moment to never live for myself again but to commit the rest of my life to God.

So as we dive into this book, I want to ask you to examine yourself. Where are you at with the Lord? This is not a feel-good, motivational book to hype you up for Jesus. Although I hope you are inspired to follow Him, I will call on you to die to yourself. I will beg you to die before you die. I will provoke you to lay it all down for Him because He is the only one who is worthy.

Each chapter describes the process I went through to take the next leap of faith and the wild ride of faith I've been on with Jesus in hopes that you will be encouraged to take the same leap of faith that I did in 2016. I will share my journey of quitting as God's employee and returning to His house as a son. I have counted the cost and found Jesus worthy of my life.

2

Escaping a "But First" Life

As a kid, my dad would ask me to do something with him, but if I was in the middle of playing I would say, "In a minute!" However, if you're anything like me, you know that a minute is never just a minute unless it's something you really want to do. So the majority of the time, I missed out on an opportunity with my dad. Sometimes it was a fun activity; sometimes it was a chance to help out with chores, but no matter what we did, I had a chance to spend time with my dad. As a young boy, I didn't always see the value in those moments because I was caught up in what I was doing. As I've gotten older, I've grown to appreciate my time more than anything else.

I was once playing my PlayStation 2 when my dad asked me to help him in the yard. As usual, I said something like, "Sure, Dad, just a second." However, I was so wrapped up in my game that I ended up playing inside for quite a while. I walked outside after realizing what had happened as my dad finished up the yard. I was so upset that I had let him down, and he had done everything by himself. If only I had walked outside right away, I would've felt so fulfilled, I would have worked hard, and I would have spent some quality time with my father. In moments like this, especially as a child and even as a teenager, we fail to count the cost of what will happen if we don't go when called.

In the Bible, several people counted the cost of following Jesus but didn't find Him worthy. First, Matthew 8 tells the story of a man who says to Jesus, "Let me first go and bury my father" (Matthew 8:21). One of my favorite preachers, Daniel Kolenda, says that this verse used to bother him because it seemed like such a reasonable request, yet Jesus responds, "Follow Me, and let the dead bury their own dead" (Matthew 8:22).[1] Why would Jesus not let this man simply go and bury his father before following Him? But Daniel had the revelation that nowhere in the Bible does it say that the man's father is already dead. What this man in the story is saying to Jesus is that he wanted to wait until his father passed so that he could get his inheritance. Suddenly, this exchange between this man and Jesus made much more sense.

How many people do we know—and maybe this even applies to you—who have said, "I'll follow Jesus when I'm retired and have money to travel and do everything He's asked me to do." Or maybe you've heard or even said, "I need to get promoted first so that I have a more flexible schedule. Then I can follow Jesus the way He's asked me to." There's never a convenient time to give everything to Jesus. Something in our lives will always hold us back from going all in. The enemy is always going to discourage us from making the decision to be fully devoted to Jesus.

I've heard it said that the devil doesn't care if you live for Jesus tomorrow, and how true that has become for so many. Tomorrow. But sadly, tomorrow never comes, and the decision to stay comfortable dominates the lives of many in our church pews.

Another man says, "Lord, I will follow You, but let me first go and bid them farewell who are at my house" (Luke 9:61).

Jesus responds, "No one, having put his hand to the plow, and looking back, is fit for the kingdom of God" (Luke 9:62). Again, this might seem like a reasonable request to some and an unreasonable, extreme response from Jesus. However, when we think about the idea of following Jesus, nothing else should matter. Remember, this is the same Jesus who said, "If anyone comes to Me and does not hate his father and mother, wife and children, brothers and sisters, yes, and his own life also, he cannot be My disciple" (Luke 14:26). Jesus isn't saying you actually need to hate your family and yourself but that in comparison to the love we have for Him, what we have for ourselves and the world would be hatred. This is a drastic example of the love and reverence we must have for Christ.

With this in mind, look back at the man who first wants to go see his family. The man possibly wanted to talk matters over with his friends and family and get their opinion. Whatever the reason, he clearly was not all in.

When we look at the disciples, we see a very different story. Peter literally left his father on their fishing boat in the middle of a workday to go follow Jesus. The dedication of true disciples is marked by their willingness to drop everything as His Word said and go.

I truly believe that sensual, earthly wisdom is keeping many from giving everything to Jesus. All the people above had reasons to follow Jesus. They didn't say "no," but they said one of the enemy's favorite words: *later.* If we lived with eternity in mind, if we lived with the meaning of salvation at the forefront of our thoughts, we would not hesitate when God calls us.

We were enemies of God, cut off from Him and heading to hell because of sin, yet He saved us through the death of His Son on the cross. We have been given a gift we could never earn and definitely didn't deserve. How, then, could we receive the gift but live as though we never did? How could we say that we will follow Jesus but never actually do the following, instead merely living a life of confessing? We must count the cost and determine that Christ is worthy of *more* than we could ever imagine.

When we catch this revelation, we will read the stories of those men in the Bible much differently than we might have before. We will say, "How could anyone delay in following the Christ? Yes, of course, leave your family behind and follow Him. Yes, let the dead bury their dead. You only get one life. Don't delay in following our Lord!"

We also need to attain a revelation of death in order to walk out this call from God to serve Him. Countless among us today have an intellectual understanding of God, but for too many, the distance from the head to the heart is far beyond eighteen inches; no, it stretches for miles and miles. A great disconnect exists between our view of God and the reality of who He is, who He says we are, and what that means in our lives. God has called us to be lovers: lovers of Himself, lovers of others, and lovers of ourselves.

Lovers of God

To be lovers of God is to honor and praise Him because He is worthy of these things and more. The Bible says, "Enter into His gates with thanksgiving, and into His courts with praise. Be thankful to Him, and bless His name" (Psalm 100:4). We are instructed to come into the presence of God by thanking and praising Him. These are two different actions and are equally important.

The definition of *thanking* or *thankfulness* is, "being conscious of a benefit received."[2] Thanking God looks like honoring Him and adoring Him for what He's done. We thank Him for sending His Son, Jesus, and for blessing us with the ability to become His children. We thank Him for making us right with Him, even when we deserved death and hell. We thank Him for all our blessings: our families, our passions, our abilities, and our resources. It's all from Him.

The definition of *praise* is to "express warm approval or admiration for someone or something."[3] We praise

God for who He is! We praise Him for being holy, righteous, blameless, matchless, faithful, and honest. We praise Him for being trustworthy, for being a good Father, for being our Helper, and for being awesome and far above and beyond anything else in creation. We praise Him for being the Creator, who formed everything by speaking it into existence. We praise Him for being all of the following: love, kindness, patience, long-suffering, truth, and life. Are you catching this? Thankfulness is for what He's done and what He's doing. Praise is for who He is, who He's been, and who He always will be. He is the same yesterday, today, and forever.

To be lovers of God is to love what He loves and to hate what He hates. Proverbs says, "The fear of the LORD is to hate evil" (Proverbs 8:13). Many pastors scarcely preach on this because when they begin taking sides, drawing hard lines, and standing on truth, they can lose followers. Jesus made statements that caused thousands to leave in an instant. He wasn't concerned with being liked, accepted, or even loved by man, but only with doing what the Father did and saying what the Father said.

This must be true for us as well. It is not popular to stand and declare from a pulpit that abortion is killing an innocent, unborn human being, and we, as the church and as believers, must never accept, permit, or endorse it, nor stand quietly by while the rest of the world does it either.

It is not popular to stand on a platform in front of people who are giving their tithes and offerings each week and state that homosexuality is an abomination of marriage and how we, as the church, must stand on Scripture and hold the line while the country is trying to do everything to normalize and legalize it. It is not popular to advocate for the nuclear family and two genders, and the list goes on.

But to love God is to hate what He hates. If we love, we must also hate. God loves life and, therefore, hates murder. God loves marriage and hates divorce. God loves truth and hates lying. We must adopt all these as our stances as well; otherwise, we are outside of God's truth and have mistakenly fallen into our own idea that the truth is subjective.

To be lovers of God is to spend time with Him. But it's not just as easy as that. Many of you have a stronghold that causes you to present reasons why you can't spend quality time with God. I need to tear that down.

Think back to the garden of Eden. When Adam and Eve sinned by disobeying God, they were cut off from relationship with Him. Adam and Eve were in perfect communion with God, fellowshiping with Him daily. Sin entered and divided them, and thus every man and woman from that point was born with a God-sized hole in their hearts, only to be filled by their Creator Himself. We are temples for the Holy Spirit, but without being filled and sealed for the day of redemption by His Spirit, we walk around empty, up for grabs by any willing spirit that we allow access.

Sadly, the world does not understand this, and their temples are filled, polluted, and defiled by demonic spirits that seek to steal, kill, and destroy but that camouflage themselves as attractive. Sin always seems attractive, but the Bible makes it clear that sin leads to death.

I am willing to bet even some of you reading this know exactly what I'm talking about. You've pursued sin because of its allure, but when the hook sank in and you realized you were caught, the bait you sought was nothing more than a decoy to a life of bondage with Satan on the other end of the line. Only the blood of Jesus can get you off that hook before you're fully reeled in.

If the world knew this, they'd quickly flee from all plans of the enemy. They'd run into the arms of the Father who created them and loves them. You see, this is what you were created for. You were created by God, for God. You were always meant to be with God. Even His only Son, Jesus, prayed this prayer in the garden: that we would be one with Him as they were one. (See John 17:22.)

The enemy uses the things of the world and attempts to distract and entice us by pulling on the desires of our flesh, which are sinful in nature. You cannot spend time in intimacy with God if you are more concerned or captivated by the things of the world. The Bible says three things will keep you from God: "For all that is in the world—the lust of the flesh, the lust of the eyes, and the pride of life—is not of the Father but is of the world" (1 John 2:16).

Why am I going into such detail about intimacy with God? Because you may not know how many "but firsts" keep you from time with God. You think it's your busy schedule. You think it's because of your kids. You think it's because you've never been much of a pray-er or a reader, and the Bible just isn't that interesting. As hard as you've tried, you can't get into it. Maybe you've thought about waking up a little earlier and giving God the first-fruits of your day, but the devil told you (or maybe it was your analytical mind) that you needed eight hours of sleep to properly function. I'd rather have six hours of sleep and time with God than eight hours of sleep and no time with Him. You can't spend more time with God because you've been deceived to believe there are more important or more entertaining things to do or better uses of your time.

Why is it that when you finally decide to stop and pray or sit with the Lord for a while, you get the urge to complete all those household chores or comb over that to-do list and see what you could do? Where did this newfound energy come from, and why does it always appear when you're ready to spend time with God? Or maybe it's the opposite for you. Maybe every time you sit down to be with the Lord, you get very sleepy and need a quick nap. You are under the influence of your flesh or the lies of the enemy, and you've been deceived for far too long.

I'm here to sound the alarm in your life. The devil has been warring for your attention because he knows that if you were to spend real time with God—not just grabbing a few minutes here and there or in your car on the way to work—you'd actually realize what it meant to be a Christian. And if you realized what it meant to be a Christian and the authority you have in Christ, you'd be able to tell that dumb ole devil to leave in the name of Jesus. When your eyes are opened to the ways the enemy has been working to keep you bound, you'll be able to go all in for Jesus.

Going All In

Going all in doesn't mean you have to quit your job and become a street preacher like John the Baptist. It doesn't mean you have to leave your career, your sport, your band, or your business to become a traveling evangelist or a missionary to the nations. What it does mean is using these places as mission fields to share and demonstrate the gospel. The call to every believer is what Jesus said that anyone who wants to follow Him should do: denial of self. Dying to self every day is the only way we will walk in freedom and the only way to truly go all in for Christ.

Think back to those stories you just read. Why did each person fail to follow the call of Jesus? Self-interest kept them from saying yes. If they had made a practice of, a devotion to, dying to self and denying self every single day, nothing would have held them back. When you are dead to yourself, you aren't alive for yourself anymore. I know that sounds obvious when you read it, but have you ever actually pondered that reality?

If you aren't alive for yourself, then you're not in it (life) for you anymore—you're in it for Him and His glory. When this is your reality and God asks you to do something, your first thought is *yes*. I have been walking in this place of full surrender (as best as I possibly can) for more than seven years, and I've never felt better. I've given up so much in my life to follow Christ, things I will talk about later in this book, and I've still never been more fulfilled, satisfied, or joyful in all my thirty-two years of living. I want you to join me on this narrow road.

Your Next Leap of Faith

At the conclusion of each chapter, I will encourage you to take a step of faith regarding the theme we just covered. I pray you finished this chapter inspired and hopeful that God would help you in daily dying to self. I pray that a reverence for God as Lord and King comes over you so that you choose to live with eternity in mind.

My challenge for you is this: Spend five minutes per day worshiping God as the Lord. You may already have time set aside to spend with the Father; you might have a designated time for Bible reading or to get in the secret place. That's amazing! I want to ask you to add these five minutes to your day for the next thirty days. Instead of doing other things first, put God first. Watch what happens within your spirit and in your life as you take time to honor God as the Lord and King. Yes, He is our friend. Yes, He is our Father. Yes, Jesus is our brother. But how often do we sit and glorify Him with language that exalts Him as the King of kings and Lord of lords? Take five minutes for the next thirty days and declare who God is over your life and over all creation.

Pause and Pray

Maybe as you're reading this, you're already being confronted about your own life and your relationship with God. I want to stop for a moment and give you a chance

28

to make matters right. Repentance is the act of turning away from the path we are on when we recognize it's wrong and stepping onto the path God has laid out for us. Let's get with the Lord for a moment before we move on. You don't need to wait until further in the book or the end of it to have an encounter with God. Let's humbly approach Him now and believe that old ways of thinking and lifestyles that keep us from Him are going to break off. Let's devote everything to Jesus now and watch as our desires and mindsets begin to change as we put Him on the thrones of our hearts.

Father, I thank you in the name of Jesus for your power to save all who come to you. I thank you that even when I've been confused or outright rebellious, you never changed your mind about me. I thank you that your Word says that you showed me your great love for me in that while I was still a sinner, you sent Jesus to die for me. Holy Spirit, provoke me to a greater level of surrender. I pray for a wild heart encounter, where I am willing to abandon anything and everything just to follow you. I thank you that you are a good Father and will never leave or forsake me. I thank you, God, that I will never be ashamed for having faith in you. Speak to me through this book and draw me even

29

deeper into relationship with you. I ask all these things in your name, Jesus. Amen.

I want to invite you now to set this book down if you feel led and continue that prayer with God. Don't just blaze ahead and keep reading; it'll still be here when you're finished. If God is moving in your heart right now, take some time to sit with Him. The greatest joy in my life and the only source of true peace is my relationship with God. That relationship has been cultivated over the better part of the last decade, and it happened in moments when I stopped everything I was doing just to sit in His presence. If you feel that pull on your heart now, take some time to let Jesus minister to your heart. Express all your thoughts to Him and give Him space to speak into each area of your life.

3

Overcoming Distraction, Deception, and Trauma

The following chapter contains material that may be upsetting. The section titled "Burying My Men" contains descriptions of death and suicide. The section titled "War" contains graphic depictions of war.

Anyone who has walked through hard times will tell you that it's rarely a single event that pushes someone over the edge, but instead a culmination of small things that all add up to create a powerful feeling of being overwhelmed. The phrase "death by a thousand cuts" in the military describes how a particular soldier had been slowly worn down by discouragement over time.[1] As an army officer, I needed to learn and hear sayings like this so I could keep an eye out for my men who might be facing hardships, whether at home, in their personal life, or at work. On average, as of 2020, 16.8 members of the military or veterans commit suicide every single day, according to the Veteran's Administration.[2] As a leader, I had to keep an eye out for any warning signs that one of my soldiers might be at risk.

I was a brand-new lieutenant in the US Army, assigned to the 1st Special Forces Group (Airborne) in Fort Lewis, Washington. I was fresh out of Army ROTC with an aeronautics degree from the Florida Institute of Technology. Even though I had grown up in Florida for the better part of my life, I was excited at this new adventure of joining the military and moving across the country. I was ready to make something of myself and get a fresh start to be whoever I wanted to be.

I left my friends and college with a solid reputation, but during my four years there, I had not made my faith a priority. While at college, I slowly began to live the prodigal life. By the end of my senior year, I was drinking and partying regularly with my friends, sleeping around, and living entirely for myself and my flesh. I had no accountability and no relationship with God, except asking Him to help me pass my accounting final, which I thankfully did.

With my little Mustang GT packed with all my earthly possessions, I hit the road headed west, ripping across the country in that muscle car. Upon arriving in Washington, the first thing I needed to do was get plugged into a great church. I had taught myself guitar during college and wanted to try out for the worship team. Within a few weeks, I had found a church, made the worship team, and was playing on the weekends. I felt like a real

Christian for the first time in a while. Now that I was in Washington, I had this new resolve to live right. I had a tiny apartment in a small town called Lacey, just south of Tacoma, and drove over thirty minutes one way, several times per week, just to get to church for rehearsal and services. Between serving at church and my work on base, I didn't have much free time.

Before too long, I was right back in the same cycles of sin that I was living in while at college. The worst part, however, was that all my new friends were Christians as well. None of us were bad people—we all loved God and serving at church, but we also enjoyed going out and partying. I began to think that this kind of behavior was normal, because I had done it with my college friends and now did it with my church friends.

I had no concept of eternity and standing before God one day, giving an account for my actions and my life. I began to subconsciously compare myself with my friends and determine that this must be normal behavior. Over time, the emptiness of partying, drinking, and meaningless, flesh-driven relationships wore me out.

I started to feel off. I wasn't convicted, because no one around me was living a life dedicated to God, and I wasn't hearing many messages about the conviction of sin and living a holy life. No one was preaching, "But they, measuring themselves by themselves, and comparing themselves among themselves, are not wise" (2 Corinthians 10:12). I was constantly comparing myself with my church friends and thinking that I was just doing what everyone else was doing. In reality, I was, but that didn't make it right.

Burying My Men

At the age of twenty-two, I became a platoon leader in charge of seventy-six soldiers. My heart raced at the thought of leading and training them for war, as I had prepared for this over the last four and a half years in college and in my Basic Officer Leaders Course. What I wasn't prepared for was burying two of my soldiers within a year of arriving. SGT Joshua Strickland and SPC Zach Carpenter never made it to 2014. Josh was killed by so-called friendly Afghan soldiers whom our unit was training on a pistol range. One of them turned and shot four of our guys, including Josh. Zach would tragically take his own life just a few weeks later.

I wept when Josh died, even though I had only briefly interacted with him a handful of times. He was one of my soldiers, one of my men who never came home. I had spent more time with Zach as my platoon sergeant, and I had helped him work through some personal issues and saw great progress. Then, one night, I received the call and rushed to the hospital. He passed away a short time later.

I broke down when I saw my soldiers the next morning. I felt out of control and didn't know how to handle a second death. I dreaded the upcoming memorial and funeral. There's something so powerful about a military funeral: the flag-draped casket, the folding of the flag that's handed to a widow, mother, father, or family member. Watching that twice in two months was more than I could handle.

Later, the family asked me by name to fly down to California where the funeral was taking place because of the bond we had built during this whole process. My unit wasn't sure if they were going to pay the cost of the trip, and Zach's dad offered to pay for all the expenses. I was incredibly humbled. Treating people right and caring for them in a time of need speaks volumes.

My unit did end up paying for the trip, and I found myself in Oxnard, California, a few weeks later, attending Zach's funeral. Only this time, his wife asked me to hand her the folded flag. One of the hardest things I've ever done was trying to remember the line to say without choking up or crying. "On behalf of the president of the United States, the United States Army, and a grateful nation, please accept this flag as a symbol of our appreciation for your loved one's honorable and faithful service."

Prepping for War

In 2014, I began prepping to deploy to the war in Afghanistan, which was the entire reason I joined the military. As a child, I watched my father, an officer in the US Air Force, leave for work in his uniform every day, which gave me a passion to serve my country. By this point, I had been a platoon leader for a little more than a year and had already buried two of my men. The stress of performing to expectation and the weight of losing my men started to eat away at who I was, and my church service and attendance didn't seem to be enough to help me rebuild.

I moved from Lacey into a bigger apartment with a view in downtown Tacoma, walking distance from my favorite bar and only a few minutes from church and work. When life got tough and circumstances went wrong, I found myself walking down to that bar a little more frequently. When life went well, I'd be down at that bar, celebrating with some friends. I attempted to escape my building depression by going out. The only time I felt as if anything could penetrate the dark cloud that hung over me was when I was drinking with my friends or playing guitar or drums at church. Even then, it was only a temporary fix, and as soon as it was over, the darkness again overwhelmed me. I was spending my free time fulfilling all the desires of my flesh but feeling more and more empty as the days went by.

In this season of ups and downs and emotional instability, I could only focus on one thing: my upcoming deployment. I was dropped off at Fort Lewis to catch a plane for Germany on my way to Afghanistan. An excitement and nervousness came over me that I hadn't experienced before. At this point, I began to fall into the trap of "I'd rather feel pain than nothing at all." What a demonic, sensually charged statement that is! Nevertheless, it was proving true in my life.

I had become so numb from the back-and-forth—fired up for God on Sundays, fired up for the world on the weekends, and emotionally drained every other day of the week. My spiritual life was dead, only to be momentarily revived by the hype of a Sunday experience, as we called them.

The idea of going to war and possibly dying for my country actually held a strange sort of appeal. I didn't realize it at the time, but looking back, I can see how I was beginning to feel the weight of real depression. At the time, I thought I was just working through some issues. But I was carrying the overwhelming weight of life on my shoulders, and it affected the decisions I made.

Luke 15 tells the story of the prodigal son. This boy had everything he could have ever needed in the house of his father, but he saw through the wrong lens because of the desires of life. As a result, he took his inheritance and departed for the city to live it up and take in all he could. One day, after indulging in the world and getting everything that sin could offer, he found himself broke and alone. This boy goes from the highest of highs to the lowest of lows. The fantasy he'd imagined at his father's house became his reality, but as with all sin, the road came to an end.

Some of you reading this right now have lived this out. You set out to pursue your fleshly desires. Sometime later, you were living out those dreams and engulfed in sin and the world; maybe you're there right now. But those of us who have walked this road before can tell you that the road always comes to an end. The story of the prodigal is the story of us all. The question is, what happens when you reach the end? Is there redemption for your life? In the world or with man, maybe not. Your reputation could be tarnished, your integrity could be forever questioned, and your name could be tainted. You may not recover from what you've said and done. However, in Christ, there is power. There is redemption. There is no condemnation. The Bible says that every one of your sins is not only forgiven but erased—forgotten entirely. The end of self is where eternal life begins, but only if you are willing to receive it.

War

My time in Afghanistan would mark me and become a point in life that I still think and speak about today. I wasn't a frontline gunner or a combat medic but was blessed to serve with the elite Green Berets as a logistics officer. I conducted logistical convoys, which are large movements from our camp out to smaller camps from which the teams would live and operate. During these movements, I manned the M240B machine gun in an open turret in the rear of an RG33 vehicle. I was thankful to have a job where I got to experience the country and get outside the wire—which was why I joined the military—as opposed to sitting on a base all day.

During my time in country, I thankfully never had to pull the trigger of my weapon, although the teams we supplied did eliminate hundreds of terrorist threats. During one mission, a rocket narrowly missed our convoy and exploded a short distance away. The flash nearly blinded me as the heat of the shock wave immediately hit my face as it passed by our trucks. We didn't have time to get down for cover. Thankfully, no one was hurt, and no vehicles were hit.

During our scan of the area, no enemies were located, and the point of origin of the shooter was never located. Often, the enemy would pop out from a building, fire a rocket at a convoy, then quickly disappear. Usually, if the hit was successful, it was followed up by an ambush of more fighters and heavy gunfire. If it missed, the enemy didn't want to further expose their position and refrained from engaging again.

Between this incident and the 155 rocket and/or mortar attacks we took on our camp alone, I was operating under a huge amount of stress. But I didn't realize it until I got out of that environment. I couldn't see how conditioned I was to respond to certain things in certain ways until I was out of it.

Near the end of my trip, I was flown by helicopter to a larger base that had shops and even restaurants. These little treats seemed like delicacies to me because our camp had none of that. I began to see a different side of deployment, where some people spent their workdays on a large, protected base, eating meals at restaurants, and buying snacks and drinks at the local shops. We didn't have the privilege of enjoying these things where I was, and the men I supported had even less than I did. Some of my friends who served overseas had little to nothing and even had to burn their own feces. Imagine for a moment not having the most basic of comforts, such as a toilet or running water. Some of our soldiers faced these conditions.

Because of my experiences, I began to get bitter toward people who didn't understand what we had been through. My anger was even more fueled toward those who talked about how easy deployment was or joked, "The war's over!" But just weeks earlier, I was scrubbing human flesh off pieces of equipment we collected after a solider from one of our teams got blown up. No, the war was *not* over.

My personality was changing, and my tolerance for people was lessening as my heart grew colder and hardened toward those in ignorance. I had no mercy for them and even less grace. The worst part was, I was justified. Oh, how horrible when you can justify your sin and when most of the world would agree with you. I'm so thankful that Christ came in and destroyed my hardness, but that would take another eighteen months.

I returned home after six months and tangibly knew I was not the same person who left back in April. A spirit tried to attach itself to me, and I unknowingly allowed that to happen. I believe that PTSD is a spirit. This does not mean that it cannot be a medical condition as well. I absolutely believe it is medical, based on the research and studies done specifically on veterans and police, as well as on victims of trauma.

However, I believe PTSD is similar to an addiction. An addiction begins with temptation. As the craving is fed, the habit forms. Over time, such as with alcohol or drugs, the brain is reprogrammed, which leads to chemical dependency. What began as a spiritual battle actually became a physical issue because the person is now chemically addicted. You can see it in a brain study.

Similar to this, I had a strange perspective upon returning to the United States. I sunk into this state of mind with the following thoughts:

- *No one knows what you've been through.*
- *You've seen so much trauma.*
- *You could have died.*
- *You were rocketed so many times.*

These were not statements from God but from the enemy. The purpose was to get me to come into agreement with them so that I would take these on as my identity.

I found myself dwelling on these things while back at home. While my friends talked, I sat in a chair and stared off into the distance, reliving my time in Afghanistan. In the middle of a conversation, I daydreamed of the war. I then had this urge to go back and even messaged my commanders that I wanted to go on the next trip to Iraq. At that time, in 2014, the war in Iraq was gearing up on a larger scale, and I wanted to be a part of it. I'd been home for a week, and I was trying to go back. It's not because I was some heroic military guy; I was oppressed by a spirit. I felt like a foreigner in my own body, which transferred to my friends and even my own country. I felt misunderstood and out of place.

For the record, I fully believe that because of the repetitive rocket attacks and times when our incoming-fire alarm went off, I was conditioned to respond to loud noises or alarms and similar stimuli. These things were not spiritual. But a practical, psychological, and even chemical reaction occurs as purely the result of exposure.

However, conditioning to loud noises and experiencing PTSD are very different. PTSD refers to mood swings, highs and lows, happiness and depression, attachment and detachment issues, and many more. PTSD begins as a spiritual issue, just like I believe depression and anxiety begin as a spiritual issue. Eventually, it becomes a chemically, physically diagnosable problem that is recognizable in the body, but by the power of God, people can be delivered from those spirits long before that point is ever reached. I had no idea of any of this, and so began the next eighteen months that nearly led to my destruction. As Scripture says, "My people are destroyed for lack of knowledge" (Hosea 4:6).

It wasn't long before the darkness I'd allowed to build inside me reared its ugly head, and I was forced to face my issues. No amount of prodigal living could fill my emptiness, and God met me and saved me at my lowest point. God encountered me when loss was the greatest, addiction was the strongest, and the value of my own life felt at its lowest. When I reached the end of myself, I had no more walls up. My defenses were down, my ears were wide open, and I was exposed. In this place, God met me and changed me forever.

Your Next Leap of Faith

Even though you may not have been in war or been responsible for soldiers, your symptoms of distraction, deception, or trauma may still be similar to mine, and you don't know how to get out. In a moment, we're going to pray for supernatural breakthrough, but I have learned one thing about getting freedom: It means being transparent. I had a small group of friends whom I trusted. I could tell them anything. Later, when I encountered God, I realized that I could tell Him anything and that He cared to listen. I want to challenge you to take a leap of faith right now and begin to tell God and a trusted friend what you're going through. Don't suffer in silence and don't allow the enemy to lie to you so that you isolate yourself.

I challenge you to talk to God every time a thought comes to your mind that doesn't produce life. Every. Single. Time. The Bible tells us that we should be "casting down arguments and every high thing that exalts itself against the knowledge of God, bringing every thought into captivity to the obedience of Christ" (2 Corinthians 10:5). Notice how it says *every* high thing. Don't allow these thoughts to fester. Don't let them sit there unchecked. Take each one to God and make an exchange, an exchange of the truth of His Word for the lie you're being fed. Exchange His peace and joy for your pain and sadness. Over time, you will see your heart and mind begin to heal as you grow in your trust of Him more and more.

I also challenge you to take a leap of faith by finding a friend you can check in with once a week or so as to how you're doing with taking these thoughts captive. Ask your friend to keep you in prayer, and if you can meet in person, have them lay hands on you, bless you, and encourage you to keep fighting the good fight of faith. You can and will always overcome as long as Christ lives in you and you are yielding to Him.

Pause and Pray

The Bible says, "For the weapons of our warfare are not carnal but mighty in God for pulling down strongholds" (2 Corinthians 10:4). This means that the tools we use to fight our battles are not what most would think, because our battles are not what we are used to. Our battles as Christians are against unseen enemies.

There's a story in the Bible about a man named Daniel, who was praying and fasting for a dream interpretation. After twenty-one days, an angel visited him and told him that they were delayed because they were fighting demons and rulers of demonic kingdoms and needed assistance. What? This is the reality we are living in as Christians.

Our eyes must be opened to the fact that there is an unseen world, a supernatural realm, where battles are being fought at all times. As Christians, we know that the war has been won by Christ, and in Him we have the victory, but we have the privilege of partaking in battles as believers in Him. The way we win these battles is by having faith, even when the enemy and the world give us thousands of reasons not to. As we pray, I want you to understand that we are taking ground in the spiritual realm. We are pushing back demonic kingdoms and rulers over principalities. In your own life, you have the ability to take territory for the kingdom of God through prayer. Whether you're facing intrusive thoughts, depression, anxiety, or any other lies, we combat them all the same way: by speaking the truth. Let's pray.

Father, I thank you in the name of Jesus for the opportunity to come to you in prayer. I thank you that by your Son, I have direct access to you. In this moment, overwhelm me with a revelation of your love for me. Thank you that you know me, you see me, and you love me. Thank you that your Word says I will never be ashamed for believing in you. Thank you that you will never leave or forsake me. I ask that you free me completely from every lie of the enemy. I bind every spirit that would bring intrusive thoughts of shame, guilt, condemnation, anxiety, depression, and even suicide, and I command them to leave in Jesus's name.

I thank you, Holy Spirit, for revealing yourself to me right now and comforting me. I thank you, God, that you did not leave me without power but gave me the gift of your Spirit to overcome every accusation of the Enemy. I thank you that I will always overcome as long as I follow you, and I pray for the courage to take my next leap of faith today despite the attacks that have come against me. I pray all this in Jesus's mighty name. Amen.

Scanning the ridgeline for enemies near Baraki Barak.

Manning the M240B machine gun during a convoy. We conducted these movements regularly to visit different Special Forces outposts that we supported.

I spent many hours in this turret!

My interpreter and I listening to enemy chatter prior to taking off on a mission. We had a device that scanned enemy frequencies and allowed us to hear them talking on their radios. On this particular day I remember them discussing our movements, size, and direction of travel. I was nervous as this would potentially be my first time engaging the enemy. Thankfully, nothing came of it, and everyone was safe.

My first week in Afghanistan on my first mission. As a new lietuenant, I was just thankful to actually be there and serve my country. I had no idea what lay ahead for me.

4

Reaching the End of Self and Finding God

Now back from the war and beginning to reintegrate myself into society, I could see the effects of the last six months on my personality manifest in several different ways. First, I was short tempered in certain situations. Any patience I used to have was on a very short fuse. My patience for loved ones and close friends hadn't changed, but I had no mercy for anyone else. They didn't know what I had seen and been through. They were arrogant and ignorant, taking for granted the privileges we have as Americans. They didn't know the true cost of the sacrifice of freedom. They didn't know the oppression of people in countries on the other side of the world. That was how I viewed those around me.

I so easily got into this head space because my eyes were fixed on self. Have you ever considered this? Maybe you are familiar with this thought pattern where everyone else is the problem. This is described in the Bible as someone whose eye is not single. When your eye is single, when it is fixed on the light that is Christ and the faith, your whole body is flooded with light (Matthew 6:22). However, if your eye is fixed on darkness, the Bible teaches that your whole body will be flooded with darkness. This is a key teaching that we need to spend more time on. Many believers think that they have tons of problems when, in reality, it might just be this one thing. When your eye is not on Jesus, your whole perspective is off. When your eye is not fixed on the Light of the World, you begin to see from a perspective of darkness, which taints your vision and reality.

I encountered a certain type of people as a rookie cop working the night shift. They were the 1 percent of the population that you wouldn't want to run into alone. They were the people who were out committing heinous and felonious, violent crimes. After weeks, months, and years of dealing with these kinds of people, if you're not careful and well-balanced, you'll begin to see the world this way. You'll begin to believe that the world is as bad as your experience each night.

Clearly, America is not as bad as a crime-infested city at three o'clock in the morning, but if you're not keeping your eyes on truth, you'll begin to feel that way and live as if it is. Living by feelings, emotions, or experiences is dangerous because the foundation is based on what you've seen and heard. Living by truth is based on what is true, what is actually real. Real and feel are different. Senior officers at my job encouraged people to take a few day shifts to balance out and interact with normal people.

My last year as a cop, I worked the day shift, and my police experience was 100 percent different. I dealt with soccer moms driving a little too fast and businessmen who turned without looking and rear-ended someone. The previous four years of my career, I was chasing stolen cars, getting into foot chases and fights with robbery or assault suspects, and pulling out my gun multiple times a night and my rifle at least once a week, just to give you a few examples. Switching to the day shift felt like a career change.

I thank the Lord that I was grounded in my faith and allowed Him to pour into me every day, because I saw that my view of people didn't change when I made the switch. I still valued people. I still saw them for who they could be, not for what they were doing. As a cop, I had to address what people were doing, but as a Christian, I remembered who they were created to be. If only I had this revelation during my time after the war, my life wouldn't have been in such turmoil. But I hadn't encountered the Lord yet and still wasn't aware of His love for me, let alone others.

Just before the war, I took a position as a wrestling coach at Wilson High School in Tacoma. I was proud to be a Wilson Rams coach and worked with my friend Josh. After the war, I needed something to pour my guts into, so the team got all of me. I don't know about you, but when life used to get me down, I'd pick a hobby, a sport, or another outlet and run after it as hard as I could. Although it wasn't the healthiest way to cope, I used it to keep my head above water. In this season, it was working out and coaching wrestling.

I had a great schedule at my new unit that allowed me to leave around 2:00 p.m. every day to make it to practice by 2:30 p.m. I grew to love the team, the kids, and Josh, and I worked hard to produce state champions. I'm proud to say we won a few tournaments, sent a bunch of kids to the state qualifier and one to the state finals. One champion even went on to win multiple state titles.

Even so, I would go home from practice or from a tournament and feel this void that I couldn't seem to kick. In my rational mind, I could not figure it out. I was serving at church faithfully every week. I was fulfilling all my responsibilities at work, loved by my soldiers and command team, and excelling at everything I did. I was staying in shape, working out for hours a day, and was coaching and giving those kids my best. I was partying with my friends on the weekends and some weeknights, heading downtown for a few drinks and conversation, but I still felt empty.

I thought about what I was missing from my life and determined that it wasn't a wife because I just couldn't seem to meet the right girl. (Who knew that good Christian girls didn't hang out at bars?) So I bought a motorcycle and got my endorsement for my license. I cruised around the PNW, through the Cascade Mountains, up to Mount Rainier, around Ruston Waterfront, and anywhere else I could. Even with the wind in my face and the beautiful scenery, I couldn't find what I was looking for. I examined my life and couldn't see what was missing. I had just closed on my first home, a new five-bedroom, 2,400-square-foot house in Tacoma. I had a straight pipe, race-tuned Mustang GT in the garage, a Jeep Wrangler in the driveway, the new motorcycle, money in the bank, friends, success, and everything I had worked for that I thought would satisfy me. But it didn't.

One night, I had driven my bike over to my buddy's house to watch a football game. While there, I got a phone call from my best friend, John. We had met in 2011 at an ROTC training event and instantly became close. I had visited him during his training in Fort Benning, Georgia, in 2012, and we were in Afghanistan together as well. We were both planning on getting out of the army to become police officers, and I was entertaining the idea of moving near Buffalo, where he was from, so that we could be partners. It was a dream, and I was about a year away from it becoming a reality.

He was my closest friend, although I didn't get to see him as often as my local friends. You know when you meet someone, and you feel as if you were siblings separated at birth? That was us. When I broke up with my longtime college girlfriend, John was so upset for me that he told his girlfriend at the time, Julianne, that she needed to call me and help me through it. I had never met Julianne, but suddenly, I was processing this breakup with her because John felt as if she could help. I never asked him to do that; he just did it. That was John. He had such a huge heart for people, which made him such an incredible leader in the army.

When I picked up the phone and said, "Hey, bro, what's up?" I was greeted by his now wife, Julianne.

She was crying and told me that John was in a really bad accident. He was in the rear vehicle of a military convoy, driving on the highway in New Jersey, when a car side-swiped his Humvee and sent them off the road.

I got all the information I needed, cleared the time off with my boss, and got on the next flight out of Seattle to New Jersey. As I rode my motorcycle home that night with tears in my eyes, I just wanted to crash it and die. I was in this strange place of knowing that I should pray for him but being furious with God for letting this happen. How could God protect us in the most dangerous part of Afghanistan for so many months and then allow this to happen in New Jersey? I screamed at God the whole way home. The sky seemed to be extra black and dark that night, and I could barely sleep, thinking about my friend in the ICU on the other side of the country.

I arrived in New Jersey in time to see my friend for a few days, even though he was in a coma the whole time. I didn't know the extent of his injuries and held on to a naïve belief that he would recover, even apart from a touch from God.

After four days, I flew back home and touched down in Seattle to a message from Julianne that John had died while I was in the air. She would later ask me to hand her the folded flag at the military funeral, an honor and privilege I had been blessed and cursed with before. I'd attended my fair share of military funerals, heard the bagpipes, seen the folded flag handed to the weeping widow, and heard the 21-gun salute, but this time, that flag represented my best friend, and I was handing it to his wife.

This began a downward spiral in my life that would take me to the depths of my soul and the end of myself: more parties, more failed relationships, and more obsessive behaviors just to try to feel something. Nothing was enough, and for the first time in my life, I didn't care if I lived. I wanted to be dead. I needed a new life but had no idea how to get it.

Encountering God

In a moment, my entire life changed when God revealed Himself to me as I sat in the booth of a local restaurant in Tacoma. God desires all of us to experience His love in a way that changes us for eternity, and I share my encounter in detail here in hopes that you'll seek to encounter Him too. The same God who appeared as a burning bush to Moses or as a thundering voice to Saul (who later became Paul), wants to make Himself known to you too. As you read my story, I pray that a desire to encounter God for yourself fills you, whether or not you know Him.

When I finally reached a point where I didn't care about my life anymore, I was empty enough for God to make a grand entrance. My mind was so full of careers, possessions, relationships, and all things self—the good and the bad—everything except God. I was scrambling and doing everything I could to create some type of order in my life of chaos and disorder. I was still attending church and serving on the worship team, but my mind was always elsewhere. I had no clue that shortly, I would have a radical encounter with the living God that would change my life forever.

In January 2016, I was preparing to exit the military and enter the police force. I had already been interviewing with several departments in the area and had submitted my paperwork to separate from the army. In that strange season, I had always thought I would be a career military man. I'd worked hard in high school and college to become an army officer. I'd worked hard in my career up to this point to set myself up for success, and now I was leaving. I believe the Lord told me to separate, because everyone else thought I was crazy for doing so. I even thought I was crazy! I didn't have a relationship with God, but I could sense that this was what I was supposed to do.

Around this time, I had become interested in a girl from my church and started hanging out with her. We went out to lunch or dinner, sometimes with friends, and on one or two occasions just the two of us. I was in such a weird place in my life that I wasn't sure what I wanted, but I was happy to have a friend with a pure heart who was unlike me in so many ways.

On January 23, 2016, we went out to eat. I sat down and opened a menu, thinking it would be a calm evening of light conversation, some food, and probably a chocolate-chip-cookie skillet, which this place was known for. I looked at the menu when my friend said, "Hey, Shane." I looked up, and she continued. "You think you're this awesome paratrooper, wrestling coach, worship drummer, and lifter, but you're not. I'm not even sure that you're actually a Christian." My jaw dropped as I was completely caught off guard. I was now sure that I wouldn't be ordering any food any time soon.

She began to preach the gospel to me for hours, telling me truths that I'd never heard in church. She told me that Jesus died for me because He loved me, not because I was some wretched sinner. Whether it was my Baptist roots or my immaturity, I had never heard a single sermon being preached to me in my twenty-five years of church attendance where I felt the way I felt that night. To this day, I haven't forgotten that feeling.

I was so aware that God really loved me. I always *knew* intellectually that God loved me because the Bible says He does, but I had no personal revelation of that love. The result of that was a life lived for self with an intellectual knowledge of my Creator, not a personal and intimate one. My friend continued to tell me that Jesus chose the cross because I was the joy set before Him (Hebrews 12:2). I grew up thinking Jesus *had* to die because I was a horrible person. I had the mentality of "look at the cross, look at what your sin did to Jesus." I couldn't understand why God loved me so much, because I was so aware of my sin, not of my value to Him.

I was crying while sitting there as the truth was hitting my heart. As if that were not enough, she then began to tell me about miracles. What? I had never seen a miracle in my life. I had never watched a person get prayed for in church for healing. In twenty-five years, I had never seen the power of God in my church. I had heard one or two stories from pastors about far-off missionaries in third-world countries who saw miraculous things, but I had never heard anything like this in the United States and never in church.

My friend said several things I will never forget, including telling me about miraculous healings as she prayed for people. The moment she said this, this light, like a spotlight that did not exist, came from the ceiling. It shone directly into my chest. As this happened, the tangible presence of God entered my body, and I immediately burst into tears. I cannot describe how I felt in that moment, but something had changed. I was incredibly aware that God was real. I told my friend that I needed to go home and rushed out the door.

At home, I found an old Bible at the bottom of my sock drawer. John's grandmother had given it to me at his funeral, and it had never been opened since then. I sat on my bed and said, "God, I realize that I've been calling myself a Christian for twenty-five years, but I've never lived a single day for you. I've lived for myself my entire life." I was having a clear and intense revelation that I was a sinner and had selfishly stewarded a quarter century of living while professing Jesus the whole time. I was guilty before the Lord. But then the tangible love of God flooded over me. My sin consciousness left, and I was overwhelmingly aware of the love that God had for me. I continued praying. "God, I have memorized so many verses of this book, but I don't even know what all it says. I don't even know where to begin. Please speak to me."

Weeping, I opened my Bible to the first page where John's grandmother had written a note. "To my beloved grandson, John. Start in the book of John. He was Jesus's closest disciple." I began to weep even harder, because God was speaking to me. I missed my friend very much, and the sentimentality of all this was touching in itself. But far above sentiment, I had asked God where to start reading, and here was a note about where to begin.

I had no idea that this was merely the start of a life of hearing God's voice for more than where to begin reading, but who to marry, what to do for a career, and much more. This was the first day I knew that God actually speaks. When I look back on my life, I can see that He always spoke; I had just never sat down to listen. Sometimes, people come into your life for a season, and then they're gone forever. I'm thankful for that girl who was bold enough to confront me in my sin and share the good news with me. I don't know where she is or what she's doing, but I'll never forget that life-changing conversation at the restaurant, which led to my salvation.

Christianity Is More Than a Prayer for Heaven

I'm so thankful for the power of the gospel to save and transform me. I was stuck in a vicious cycle of self-destruction, addiction, and sin that, coupled with a seared conscience, made for a life that had no prospect of becoming anything of value to the kingdom of God. When I sat down on my bed that night and reflected on my life, I was amazed at how all my decisions were selfishly motivated. Sure, I did things that were honorable and noble, such as joining the military, going to war, becoming a police officer, serving on the worship team, etc. The problem, though, was that all these decisions were made because that was what *I* wanted. Every single decision in my life—where to go to school, what career to pursue, where to live, what house to buy, and even what friends to have—was chosen by me. I presented nothing to God and didn't even have a grid for His input.

God began to father me that night as I sat alone at midnight with my open Bible. He began to show me how, even in my selfishness, He never changed His mind about me. He showed me that He used all those things for my good, which led to the encounter at the restaurant, which turned my heart toward Him forever. God showed me what I had been striving for all along: acceptance, love, and validation, to name a few. These were really efforts to find Him. He showed me why I was never fulfilled by the things of the world, no matter how intense the experience or how much I attained. I was climbing the ladder at work with no satisfaction in sight. I owned the house, the cars, the bike, and the dog and had money in the bank, and it didn't fulfill me. Mark 8:36 says, "For what will it profit a man if he gains the whole world, and loses his own soul?"

That night on my bed, God took me to the end of my life and let me look back on it. I had a perspective that I had never once considered before: I had attempted to gain the world, but at what cost? The condition of my soul was deteriorating even though I spent ten to fifteen hours a week in a church, leading worship. God showed me that there was more to the Christian life than church attendance and trying not to sin. He showed me that what I was now doing on my bed in secret when no one else was around, just talking to Him from my heart, was actually why Jesus died and what He paid for. God showed me that I deeply desired intimacy, and for the first time in my life, I was engaging in it. I had an aha! moment on that bed, and I vowed to never go another day without sitting with the Lord in intimacy.

Maybe you're reading this and identifying with what I'm saying. Maybe you're knee-deep in sin, living for yourself, with no heart for God. You might say your heart is for Him. I sure did, but your life will actually prove what you believe. The good news is that if you identify with the first half of my testimony, the second half is available to you. My story is not a one-off or an exception. I am not some chosen man of God with special privileges, set apart for things that you weren't.

No, in fact, the Bible says the following about all of us: "For whom He foreknew, He also predestined to be conformed to the image of His Son" (Romans 8:29). That means *all* of us were predestined, chosen by God before the world was even created to become His children. God's will for my life and yours, when the earth was formless and void and the Spirit was hovering over the waters, was always for us to be His children.

I didn't understand this until January 23, 2016, when I said yes to Him. The Bible says we love God because He first loved us (1 John 4:19), and on that night, I encountered that love. I had not experienced a lot of religion in my twenty-five years in the church. On the contrary, I also experienced communities that didn't like religion and, as a result, preached comfortable messages that kept people returning each week but never cut to the heart.

When Peter preached to the very people who killed Jesus, they were cut to the heart and asked the question that still is asked today as a response to the preaching of the true gospel: "What must I do to be saved?" (Acts 2:37). I'm so thankful for my friend, who cut to the heart with a message of conviction and love, which opened the door to my repentance. Since that night, I told the Lord that I never wanted to preach a message that didn't confront people with the truth of God and provide an opportunity to repent if needed.

If you are reading this and you recognize that you need to give your life to Jesus, I want to give you an opportunity to do that right now. The Bible says that your mouth confesses what your heart believes (Romans 10:9), and right now, you may be feeling a stirring inside and a compelling to confess to God your sin and belief in Him and give your life to Him. If that's you, I want you to lay this book down and get real with God. No one led me in a prayer that night, and to be honest, I didn't need to be led. When truth hit my heart, I knew I was guilty before God, had never lived for Him, and needed Him desperately. I responded to Him from my heart and gave Him my life. Wherever you're at right now, I invite you to do the same. The man in Acts 16 asked, "What must I do to be saved?" Peter answered, "Believe on the Lord Jesus Christ, and you will be saved, you and your household" (Acts 16:30–31). And this is my answer to you.

After that night, I was forever changed. I didn't know what lay ahead for me. I had no clue that I would soon meet my wife, enter intense spiritual warfare for several years, almost lose my life, see mighty miracles, preach all over the nation, leave the police force in a radical leap of faith, and all the rest that God would see me through. All I knew was that I hated my old life, and I was so thankful to have a new one, to be walking with God. I opened that Bible to the book of John and began to read.

Your Next Leap of Faith

I want to challenge you to step out in faith by taking some risks. Maybe you know someone like the Shane I was before I met Christ. What if, led by the Spirit of God, you had a heart-to-heart discussion with someone you care about who isn't living for God? What if, led by love in your heart, you shared the gospel with them and helped them see that they might be living a life apart from Christ? What if you did this because you desperately care for them and want to see them walking on the narrow path?

Maybe you don't know God for yourself. I challenge you, I urge you, to get alone and cry out to Him. On my bed, all alone with my Bible, I began a relationship with God. You, too, can know Him if you would only just begin the conversation. Starting tomorrow, make a point to set aside alone time with Jesus. Protect this time with a vengeance.

Every Christian needs to carve out at least an hour, if not two, to sit with Jesus every day. But as you begin to shift your schedule and find a groove, at first try to give Jesus fifteen to thirty minutes. Wake up a half hour earlier than usual and sit in a quiet room with Him. Talk to Him, pray to Him, worship Him from your spirit, and love Him with all your heart, mind, soul, and strength. Do this every day and watch your life transform before your eyes.

Pause and Pray

A story like this may have created a wonder and excitement in your heart about a relationship with God. Or maybe it brought up questions you can't seem to answer right now. Regardless of where you are, the Bible says we are saved by grace through *faith*, not understanding. Faith is believing in what we cannot see, and I pray this chapter inspired you to have hope again for God to do a fresh work in you. Let's pray now and believe that He will.

God, thank you for your great love for me. Thank you that you stopped at nothing to reveal yourself to the world. From creation to Jesus Christ, you have shown your plans, your majesty, and your love for this world. I want to know your love too. I ask that I would begin to have a hope in you that I've never experienced before.

Lord Jesus, I thank you that it is your desire that none shall perish. I know that I am a sinner, and I cannot do anything to save myself. I am now ready to answer the door as you knock. By faith, I am ready to ask you into my heart and to receive you. Thank you, Lord Jesus, for coming to earth. Thank you that you died on the cross for my sins and rose from the dead on the third day. Thank you for forgiving my sins and for the wonderful gift of eternal life. Thank you for your gift of salvation. I trust you as my Lord and Savior and ask you into my heart. In Jesus's name.

I now ask you to fill me with a fresh hunger for your presence and for your Word. I ask you to fill me with your Spirit and set me on fire to walk in righteousness and be holy as you are holy. I thank you that you hear me when I pray. I pray this in the name of Jesus. Amen.

5

Moving from Walking in the World to Walking with God

Life happened pretty quickly after being born again. I began spending a lot of time with a guy named Jacob Coyne (IG @jacobcoyne), who is now one of my best friends and was the best man in my wedding. I thought he was weird when I first saw him back in 2012, because he would jump around during worship and speak in tongues during prayer.

In 2016, I had this random, overwhelming thought. *Call Jacob and tell him what happened. Ask him to hang out.* I had never talked to Jacob, and we had never hung out one-on-one, but I thought this might be God, so I obeyed. I didn't even have his number but had known his wife, Mariah, for years and had been a worship drummer on the youth team that she led. I reached out to her and asked her to link me up with Jacob because I had just been wrecked by God and I wasn't sure what was going on.

A few days later, Jacob and I were grabbing brunch at Dirty Oscars Annex in Tacoma. (I highly recommend the elk hash or chicken biscuit.) However, something better than the breakfast happened that day. As I told Jacob what was happening, his eyes lit up, and he connected with everything I was saying. He was so excited for me and began to walk me through some of what was happening.

For instance, I'd started to feel my hands tingle with what felt like electricity when I prayed. It was so intense that it was distracting, but I had no idea what it was. Jacob said, "Let's go pray in my car." So we walked outside and sat together in his car and just prayed. I felt a little strange because I had never prayed with someone one-on-one before, but I was along for the ride.

Jacob began to pray that God would use me to do miracles and that my hands would heal the sick in the name of Jesus. My hands instantly got really hot, almost burning, and that electric feeling went through them again. Then this belly laugh erupted from Jacob as I told him what was happening, and the next thing I knew, I was laughing. Honestly, I thought I was just subconsciously acting like this to try to fit in, because the laughter came out of nowhere, so I told myself I was going to stop. The harder I tried to stop, the harder I laughed. I literally couldn't stop, and it got to the point where I was asking God to make it stop because my stomach hurt.

Jacob and I sat in the front seat of his car, praying and laughing like lunatics for a few minutes before I went home, wondering what all this meant. Was this an encounter with God? I was so new to all of it that I was still quite skeptical, but my heart was positioned to believe. I couldn't deny the things I'd experienced or the lightness and freedom I felt inside me.

Over the coming weeks, I began to pray for every single sick person I could find. I approached people with canes, in wheelchairs, and with casts or crutches, and asked them if I could lay hands on them and pray. I prayed for hundreds and hundreds of people and never saw any results. I told myself that I would pray for at least ten people every day.

At that time, I was starting at the police academy, and after I finished for the day, I would drive to the grocery store or the mall by my house and prayed for the home-less. In Tacoma, the homeless situation is beyond out of control. Sadly, tents and sleeping bags are everywhere: on every sidewalk, in front of every business, and more. It's impossible to ignore.

These people were hurting and lacking and needed the kingdom of God, so I prayed for them daily. After a month or two, I had prayed for more than five hundred people and never saw one miracle or healing. As I was sitting in my Jeep in front of a Fred Meyer grocery store off Seventy-Second Street, I said something like this to the Lord.

"God, I love you, and I know that healing is for today, and it is for the believer. Your Word says these signs follow those who believe. God, I will never stop praying for the sick. Please start healing people because you're starting to look silly out there when I tell people you're going to heal them and you don't. Thank you for loving me. I'm never quitting praying for the sick. In Jesus's name. Amen."

I hopped out of my Jeep, and a man was standing right there, so close that I could've hit him with my door. He asked me if I had a few dollars. I told him, "Sure, but can I pray for you?"

He began to tell me several issues in his body, including a bad kidney, a bad knee, and a painful toe. I told him that God would heal all of it. I got down on my knees and hovered my hands around his knee so that if God touched him, he—and I—would know that it wasn't my hands. I began to pray a simple prayer.

"God, thank you for loving this man. I pray right now that his knee would be healed in the name of Jes—" when all of a sudden, he kicked his leg straight out.

"Woah!"

I jumped up and asked him what was going on, and he told me that his knee had gotten really hot. I told him to try something he couldn't do before, and he started *running around the parking lot*! He was healed! He was so excited that he asked me to pray for the other problems to be healed too. I was so overwhelmed that God had healed this man and would use someone like me to do it. I prayed for the kidney and the toe, and he testified that both areas experienced the same heat and that all pain and discomfort left his body. He then testified that Jesus Christ is Lord.

From that moment, I knew that miracles were for today, that God was a loving, caring God who healed, that He would use anyone who was hungry for Him, and that I would never be the same again. To see me interview the person who received this healing, search "The first miracle I ever saw!" on my YouTube channel.

Jesus Freak

Everyone loves the title of "Jesus freak" until it comes time to do "Jesus freak" things. I began to see miracles break out everywhere I went and recorded as many of them as I could to post on Facebook and Instagram. In my mind, if people saw a miracle or heard someone testify that God healed them (in America, nonetheless), massive revival would follow. So I began to record everyone who was willing to share after getting healed, and I posted videos on my page, believing that they would change the world.

To my surprise and dismay, no one seemed to care. To give you an idea of how little they cared, a picture of me buying my first house in 2014 got around three hundred likes, but a video of a man testifying that God healed him in the mall got around forty to fifty.

I was confused. This was the power of God at work, with firsthand accounts. These were not stories from other countries or even from the Bible; these healings had happened in our city. I witnessed them with my own two eyes, and this person experienced them in their own body, yet no one seemed to care. The only person I could tell that seemed interested was Jacob, and so for what seemed like years, we shared testimonies of what God did each day. Both of us were in the streets, praying for the sick and open-air preaching to whoever would listen in malls, stores, and other public places.

My faith grew so much in that season. I got used to sharing the gospel with one or two or five people in public. No lights, no microphone, no graphics with my picture on it, no stage, no promotion, just raw interactions with real people who needed the kingdom. I got words of knowledge and wept with the people as I shared with them. I saw the heart of God for the one.

I learned how to take risks and how to hear God's voice over the next five years by being willing to be mocked, ridiculed, canceled, and threatened—some of this by people in my own church. By this point, it didn't matter. I had seen too much to care what anyone thought about me. I had seen people get out of wheelchairs in the name of Jesus. I had seen deaf ears open. I had seen crippled hands be restored. I had seen depression, anxiety, and suicide break off people that I had just met in a park.

That's the thing about walking with God. The longer you do it, the less you care what people think about you, and the more the fire within you grows. If your body was physically set on fire, you wouldn't care what other people thought about you. It is the same principle with the Spirit of God. When set ablaze by the fire of God, the opinions of man are burned up in His presence. The more consumed you are by His fire, the less you'll care or even notice the opinions of those who try to come against you. I had no idea that this small form of persecution would intensify in the coming years, and my circle of friends would drastically shrink to just a handful of people who burned for Jesus that I truly walked with and trusted.

When I got born again, I thought that everyone would be so excited for me. I imagined my friends going, "Wow, Shane, this is amazing! I'm so happy you're on fire for Jesus!" But many didn't respond this way. In fact, even the ones who initially responded this way eventually drifted away with the rest. Walking with Jesus has its limits with many people, even inside the church. The closer I seemed to get to Him, the smaller my circle got.

Even as I type this now, the Lord said to me, "Fire doesn't burn up fire," and I saw a vision of items getting too close to a giant flame, and they began to burn. I knew that the Lord was showing me what happened to people I used to hang out with.

Now, before I go any further, I am not writing this from a position of holier than thou. Not at all. But some Christians who genuinely believe in God still limit Him. When you surround yourself with people who have limits when you do not, it quickly becomes uncomfortable. This is magnified if those around you struggle with pride or concern for their self-image. Those with no limits will constantly be doing things that might be considered embarrassing.

Before long, people won't want to be around you because you're the weird spiritual person. How about hopping up on a booth at a restaurant and preaching the gospel because the Spirit of God came over you? How about giving words of knowledge to your waiter at the beginning of the meal? What if some of the words are wrong? You'll find out if you've got an ego problem really quickly if you're embarrassed or don't want to be seen with someone like that. This was my life, and I watched people fade away over the months and years.

The End of My Army Career

As if this pruning that came as a product of my new-found love for Jesus wasn't enough, I had more to learn and walk through. Don't you just love the Lord? Sometimes you sense that you're in a trial or in a season of pressing, and you can stomach it. You can accept your reality, brace yourself for whatever is to come, and release all expectation, control, and fear by handing it over to Jesus. "Lord, I don't know what's coming next, but I know that you're with me and I'll always overcome with you. Thank you for never leaving me. I love you." That simple prayer will cover you.

However, sometimes a season of pressing takes you by such surprise and is so intense that you can't quite stomach it. You will need to learn to roll with the punches. You're on a journey with God, and there's not much more to say about it. Well, I found myself in this place at the beginning of 2016.

At the end of 2015, I had my whole life planned. I had worked for years to become an army officer, and in 2015, I had been training for the Special Forces Assessment and Selection (SFAS) program to start my career as a Green Beret. As an officer, you cannot even apply to try out for this program until you reach a certain rank. That time had come, and I had a SFAS date of spring

2016. I was working with Green Berets in my unit to prepare physically and mentally for the intense three-week selection and felt confident that I would one day earn a Green Beret and lead a team into battle.

Earlier in the book, I talked about how John and I were planning to exit the military together in the summer of 2016, when our contracts were up, and become cops together. After he died, I felt as if my life had flipped upside down. I needed something to invest my life in because I could see it coming off the rails. I was also so deeply moved by how John's men (his soldiers) spoke of him at his memorial. As I thought about my men back home, I had this strong desire to pour as much as I could into them. At that moment, at John's memorial, I decided to pursue earning a Green Beret.

I came home and began training harder than I'd ever trained for anything before. I studied all the necessary curriculum, worked out three times per day, and positioned myself to not only pass the upcoming selection but destroy it. I didn't want to enter that program, wondering if I had what it took. I wanted to walk into that process confident, not in myself to succeed, but in my preparation. I wanted to know that I know that I had done everything humanly possible to pass and ensure that I had no regrets or worries come selection time. If I was in a bad mental space, it would be because of a lack of preparation. So my life became about my soldiers and my career.

During this process, a small administrative error interrupted my promotion to captain. Due to a tiny clerical error, an official photograph had not been attached to my file, and my packet was not accepted for promotion. To give you an idea of how silly this is, the promotion to captain is nearly automatic as long as you don't have any heinous remarks on your file and haven't been arrested. Not only was I clear of any of those marks, but my packet had exceptional reviews from Green Beret commanders I had served under, both domestically and in Afghanistan.

To make a long story short, one of the Special Forces Team Leaders I served with in Afghanistan was now working for Human Resources, the department that handles all things administrative for officer careers, including promotions, and was able to get the error fixed and my photo attached without a problem. *Okay, good, we are back on track*, I thought. But right after this, God spoke to me so clearly that I couldn't miss it. (This was around November 2015, still months away from the encounter with God in the restaurant. But I *knew* it was God because it didn't make sense.)

God said, "I don't want you in the military anymore." And the strangest thing happened. Just like that, my desire to serve as a Green Beret, my desire to be a career army officer and rise the ranks to general one day, were gone. Instantly. There was no wrestle. There was no back-and-forth. It was as if my heart had already settled it before my brain could even comprehend what God said. I knew I needed to obey this instinct. I didn't hear an audible voice, but it came in the form of a thought that was directed *toward* me. I can't deny the peace that came over me after that, and for that reason, I believe it had to have been God.

78

From that moment, I began the process of testing for the police academy. I had just been training for months for one of the hardest military schools in the world, so the police entrance exam was almost laughable in comparison. God used my work ethic to prepare me to enter this new career. I aced all my tests and scored the highest in every category. I was accepted by a department and placed at the top of their list out of more than one hundred applicants. I was officially hired and given badge number 0220.

However, I'm not writing this book to tell you how awesome I performed during police testing. See, while I was experiencing God in supernatural ways and seeing His favor over my life, not everyone saw it the same way. Some people of different ethnicities at my church immediately looked at me differently because I was going to wear a police uniform. When I was in the army, I was loved. Now that I was going to be a local cop and help clean up the crime in our city, I was hated. This would be my next test.

New Uniform, New Shane

My born-again experience happened during police testing, so by the time I was officially hired on April 1, 2016, I had been walking with the Lord and seeing miracles for months. I went through the Dan Mohler School of Kingdom Living, and I gained a heart for Jesus, my own life, and for others that I never knew was possible. I learned how to hurt for people instead of because of them. I learned about the value of my life and why Jesus did what He did. I gained a reverence for the Lord that has grown to this day. I saw how God strategically placed this course in my life before I joined this profession because I would have thousands of reasons and opportunities to be offended. Without proper perspective and identity, you'll respond to offense out of the flesh, which benefits no one. Now that Christ was in me and I was dead to myself, I had thousands of opportunities to show the love of God to everyone I met, whether victim, witness, or criminal. My heart was made brand-new, and I was excited to make a true change in my city.

I wish I could say the same for everyone around me. Offense seemed to be the rising popular stance to take in regard to police. I will be the first to tell you that 2016 was not the best time to become a police officer. Four cops in Dallas had just been murdered, and more were being killed nationwide as a result of ambushes and other coordinated attacks against police. I was fed this information daily while training as a recruit in the academy. I kept hearing about how wild the city I was heading to was. People said that one year at my department on the night shift was like working ten years anywhere else. I couldn't fully grasp what they meant while sitting in a classroom, learning about tactics and case law, but I would quickly find out.

I wish I could say that a dangerous city was the only thing I had to worry about, but it wasn't. You'd think that as a cop, you'd have the support of those in your church, and for the most part, I did. But some people that I was close that said things to me like, "You'll never be my friend," and "You are the enemy." All because I changed uniforms. They failed to see the fruit of the Spirit in my life. They failed to recognize that I was still Shane, just heading to a different place for work, wearing a different uniform.

Others began to blame me for all police brutality that has ever taken place in this country, and I hadn't even graduated from the academy. I'm so thankful for the Lord, who showed me the spiritual battle that was taking place and led to me pray instead of protest.

My heart broke when I heard these comments but not because I was hurt or offended. I actually hurt for those saying these things, because I could see the condition of their heart, and it led me to weep. I've never cried for someone as hard as I did when those specific comments were said to me, among others that I won't repeat here. I could feel the evil spirit of division and of racism at work, and I wept bitterly because of how disgusting it was. I finally experienced Romans 8:26, which says,

> Likewise the Spirit also helps in our weaknesses. For we do not know what we should pray for as we ought, but the Spirit Himself makes intercession for us with groanings which cannot be uttered.

As a new Christian, I began to learn the difference between just being a believer and being a follower of Jesus. I had believed my whole life, but now I was following the man who saved me. As I followed Him, my heart and mind were transformed. A believer has intellectual knowledge of Jesus but no revelation, leaving their flesh alive and giving a large runway for offense to land. A Christian is in pursuit of Christ and daily trying to die to self to see Christ formed in them. While offense may try to grow, as they grow in their intimacy, knowledge, and revelation of Jesus, the runway grows smaller and shorter until one day, the plane of offense has no room to land and is forced to touch and go at best.

The result of this pursuit of Christ was truly being able to live unoffended when those around me lashed out. I could see the spirits at work in these situations, and because of that, I could combat that darkness with the light within me. When you recognize activities as spiritual, you will respond spiritually. How awful would it have been if I had only seen with the lens of my flesh? I would've responded with my flesh. I find that many people do, which produces no life and only creates further division and strife. We must keep our eyes on Jesus and live by the Spirit of God so that we do not fulfill the flesh and its desires, as it says in Galatians 5:16.

So while people are up in arms against the police, I am too busy praying for the sick and ministering the heart of God to my classmates, teachers, and everyone else I encounter throughout my day. It's amazing how keeping an eternal perspective and not getting caught up in the temporal will change everything. You'll become an effective Christian, not just another church attendee with a confession of Jesus as Savior but with a hundred reasons—and even justifications—as to why you're upset.

How sad would it be to live a life where you claim to follow Christ and even attend a church faithfully but look exactly like those who don't even believe? What a waste of time to sit through services week after week and even read your Bible out of religious obligation for years or even decades and not be transformed. There is more to this Christian life than warming a pew and reading a book (the Bible) as if it were history and not a river of life.

I don't say any of this to make you think I am holier than thou or that I have arrived. I know who I am without Christ, and I have seen who I am with Him, and I can tell you firsthand that I had nothing to do with that transformation. I simply yielded my life, mind, will, and emotions to God and asked Him to make much of that small sacrifice. I do my best to do this daily, as we all should, because we all are being sanctified and working out our salvation every day. I didn't wake up and *try* to be a Christian. I gave myself to Jesus and spent my mornings looking at His face in prayer and in the Word, and over time, I began to see the fruit of that reveal itself without any effort on my part to make it appear.

I said all the above because I understand that there are those who can read my testimony or hear some of these things and think that all they need to do is try harder or go *do* what I did. Maybe you've been reading this and are provoked to change. Good! But be provoked into the prayer closet. May my words never provoke someone to try to enlist themselves into God's army and become the employee of the month by all the great works they do. No, no, no. Be provoked to love. Love God, love yourself as He loves you, and love others. From that place, your heart will overflow and spill out on every part of your life.

As I loved on Jesus in secret, as He showed me who I was in Him, and as I began to love who He made me to be, I saw my outward love grow. I naturally wanted to express that love to everyone I saw. I naturally wanted to give the kingdom to anyone I saw that needed it. One morning, as I was driving to the academy, I had an impression in my spirit that someone in my class needed prayer for their knee. I had no reason to think this, and the thought came randomly as I made the drive from my house to school, so I believed in faith that God was speaking to me. I was going to go ask if anyone needed prayer.

As I entered the building, one of my classmates came into the room, limping horribly. I asked him what happened, and he told me that he had badly injured his knee during a defensive tactics training the night before. It was so bad that he was at risk of not completing the course with our class and was facing the possibility of having to recycle to the class behind us or even further back, depending on recovery time. My heart broke upon hearing this, because we all had put in so much hard work to make it this far. I imagined how devastated he was feeling at the thought that an accident might delay or even uproot his dream of becoming a police officer.

I asked him if we could quickly pray before class started, and he said yes. We prayed for less than twenty seconds, and I asked him to test out his knee. He was completely healed—all pain left, all limitation of movement was gone, and he was back to normal. He began walking around the classroom without a limp, and everyone was amazed because they had just seen him limping horribly. (Some of them were even at the training the night before, when the injury happened).

God got all the glory that morning. I didn't wake up and *try* to be a good Christian. I woke up and knew who God was and who I was and why I was alive: to shine for Him. I left my home with every intention to shine, which meant my focus wasn't on myself and having a good day, but on manifesting the presence and glory of God everywhere I went. As a result, I had an open mind to hear God speak. A man was radically healed, and many bore witness to it.

This was God's introduction to my career as a police officer. Yes, I would learn tactics and rise to the top of my class and later, to the top of my department for the great police work I did, but God showed me early on that my time as a cop would be for greater efforts than just cleaning up crime in my city. (This is already a very noble goal, and I give my utmost thanks to every past and present police officer keeping our nation safe.) How ironic that during my time in the police academy, the Lord had me going through something of a Holy Spirit Academy every morning and night on my bed in my room. My life was truly changing in every way, and I was just along for the ride. I've only scratched the surface of what God would do with these stories and testimonies and the power He would work through and in me, including a brush with death that forever changed me.

Your Next Leap of Faith

Now that we have released faith over our lives and surrendered it to God, we still have more to do. James tells us that faith without works is dead. (See James 2:14–26.) This does not refer to salvation but to our daily lives. We can sit here and read and pray and talk about faith until we are blue in the face, but moving in faith and building faith requires action and risk. We talked about this in the previous chapter. Your next leap of faith is one action away from becoming a reality.

At times, I am provoked to pray and give God something, and at times, I'm provoked to pray and then go do it. As you read about what God has done and prayed for Him to do it in you, it's time to act. Often, God is waiting on me to make the first move, and then He moves upon my faith.

Do you desire to see a change in your heart and mind, a change in your city, state, and even nation? It starts with you. This week, I want you to tell two people every day that God loves them and ask them if you can say a quick prayer for them. Ask them if they need any specific prayer; otherwise, pray a blessing over them and that they would continue to seek Jesus for truth, peace, and joy in their heart and mind. Take no more than thirty seconds (unless led by the Spirit) and pray a short prayer over two strangers every day this week. By the end of the week, you'll have prayed for at least

86

fourteen people. Imagine if you did this every week. You'd reach 730 people for Jesus every single year.

Don't discount the effectiveness of a short prayer. I intentionally said thirty seconds or less because I don't want you to be intimidated by thinking you need to pray some long, eloquent prayer. Remember, Jesus raised Lazarus by simply telling him to come out. If you have some cool testimonies, send me a direct message on Instagram @shane.winnings, and I will share them with my followers.

Pause and Pray

I'm thinking of you reading this right now and what might be going on inside your mind and heart. I know what happens in me when I hear someone's testimony. Faith is released for God to do a similar work in my life. You don't have to be in the military or in the police academy or even desire those things to experience a move of God. As you reflect on what He did for me in the last chapter and up to this point in the book, I want you to believe for Him to do those things in you as well. We are going to ask God to move upon the faith that has been stirred up in your heart.

I can confidently say that my testimony to this point has created faith because it has nothing to do with me.

Whenever a testimony of the faithfulness, goodness, and transformative power of God is shared, all who hear are pricked by the Spirit to believe. All who hear are invited by God to hope for the same and more in their own lives. It's Christ in us, the hope of glory, the hope of the glory of God to be revealed in and through us.

Do you want that in your life? I'm sure that you do. Let's pray right now and not waste this holy moment where faith is hovering, waiting to be acted upon. I've learned that whenever I feel faith come over me, the time to act has arrived. Whether I need to take a physical step or release a prayer, I need to do something. Let's engage with this gift God is releasing over you. Pray with me.

Father, I thank you in the name of Jesus for testimonies. Thank you that your Word says in Revelation 12:11 that the word of our testimony is one of the ways we overcome the enemy. God, I know you want to do something wonderful and powerful in my life. I'm not here to ask for blessings, riches, or fame. I'm here to ask you to make much of my life for your glory. I'm here to ask you to take my life and glorify yourself in and through it. I offer up my life to you right now by faith. I see what you did in Shane, and I'm asking you to do that and even more in me. Do it for me, God. Transform my heart and mind to live unoffended. Use me to work miracles and hear you speak for those around me. Help me to love you with all of my heart, mind, soul, and strength. In the name of Jesus, I pray. Amen.

6

Discovering That a Supernatural Life Is Normal Christianity

The more I began to spend time with Jesus and a couple of faith-filled believers, the more I could feel my fire growing. I wasn't doing anything special to make my fire grow, but I was being consumed by the very fire Himself. I was in proximity to the fire as much as possible, and as a result, I began to spontaneously combust and burn everywhere I went. It wasn't long before I was preaching in restaurants, colleges, grocery stores, and anywhere else people gathered. I prayed for as many people as possible whenever I could.

My mindset was drastically different than it had ever been. Before, I would be concerned about myself and how to complete the tasks I had laid out that day. Now, I was concerned about revealing my Father to anyone who would give me the time of day and preaching even to those who wouldn't. I felt like work was just something I did between my street preaching. Work began to get in the way of time I could spend praying for people or studying the gospel. Around this time, I knew one day I would be a preacher and that my career as a cop, though it was just beginning, would not last for long.

With this type of pull comes the temptation to remove your heart from your current occupation. My dad always taught me to do the best at whatever I was currently doing, even if I desired to do something else. God was calling me to do the same thing. I cannot express how badly I wanted to travel and preach the gospel and see dead or sleeping Christians, just like I had been, wake up. I wanted to tell the nation of what God had done for me and of the truth of the gospel, the truth I'd never heard but always needed. At first, I struggled to connect with my position as a police officer because God was tugging on my heart to preach.

I learned a few things in the five years that I was a cop, which helped me give my all in both ministry and in my police job and helped me not become "so heavenly minded that I'm no earthly good," as the saying goes.

The first lesson I learned was stewardship and humility. The Lord was hiding me when it came to ministry and giving me grace to excel as a police officer. During my time as a police officer, I was only invited to speak two times at churches. I felt God telling me to focus on the people in the streets and all around me, to preach on social media, and to give my very best at my job. God showed me how He cannot honor someone at a job who does not do the job with honor. Imagine how it would look to my bosses if I claimed to be this on-fire Christian and slacked at work or daydreamed because I wanted to preach instead. The Lord needed to work on some issues in my heart and develop it before He elevated me in any way in ministry.

After receiving that revelation, I stopped daydreaming about preaching and went all in on my police job. I told the Lord that I would not try to force anything when it came to ministry and that I would serve as a cop for as long as He asked me to. I also learned how to steward what was in my hand, meaning what I was currently responsible for or had access to. Street preaching and social media preaching was not only important to God, but also important for me to keep up with and treat as a real ministry. I often uploaded prayer videos, went live on Facebook or Instagram, preaching and praying for people, or live-streamed when I was out in public, praying for the sick and sharing the gospel. I didn't go out and try to do ministry.

Ministry can easily become both an idol and a goal that people think needs to be formal. This can create a weird mindset of doing ministry as a job instead of living Christianity as a lifestyle. God quickly stripped away my desire for a title or a position and began to emphasize the title of son into my heart and head. He showed me that "ministry" is simply an overflow of love for others. That love comes from a place of intimacy, which is cultivated in the secret place. God began to draw me into the prayer closet day by day, teaching me His ways and giving me His heart for others.

A natural result of that was seeing someone with a cast or cane or in a wheelchair and feeling as if it was time to go be a good Christian and pray for them to see a miracle and to give them the kingdom. I'd see someone hurting, limping, or crying, and my heart hurt because I knew what it was like to be injured, in pain, or in heartache. I just had to go over and talk to them and ask if I could pray.

God showed me how many people can accidentally fall into the mindset of using people to try out or even show off their spiritual gifts. He showed me that when you pray for someone to be healed just so that you can see a miracle or practice healing the sick, you're using them. The motivation for Jesus was always love. Paul says if we don't have love, we can heal all the sick in the world and we've still got nothing!

When love is your motive, you stay humble. As a new believer, after being born again for a few months, I was seeing miracles every single day: radical healings, giving accurate words of knowledge, prophesying, doing deliverance, all of it. It was absolutely wild, and God seemed to put me on a fast track. I learned in months what some people went to ministry school for years to do. This intense track came with temptation.

I did my best to keep my heart pure, but success repeated over time can start to make you feel successful. This made me feel as if I needed to keep it going. I never woke up thinking that on purpose, but I was suddenly facing a temptation I'd never felt before. I was so confused, and it was as if I couldn't just pray for someone anymore without thinking about their reaction, how they would feel about me, and what they would think of me. Through all of it, God fathered me. Whenever I was tempted to perform a miracle, God lovingly reminded me that I would be straying from His heart for that person. That still, small voice kept me close to Him and away from pride. It's easy to sit and read something like this and think, *I'd never act like that! I'd never try to perform!* But I never woke up with that mindset once since I've been born again. That's how pride creeps in. Pride isn't obvious, but slow and sneaky. It can happen when you've just been born again and have prayed for countless people, seen countless miracles, given incredibly accurate words of knowledge, and prophesied things over people that changed their lives.

Subconsciously, these thoughts can run through your brain, and you begin to agree with what these kind-hearted people have said. "You are amazing. You are truly being used by God. You are so anointed. You're so prophetic. You are a messenger from God. You have a gift unlike anything I've ever seen or even heard about. You're the next (insert famous minster's name)." These compliments can actually derail a baby Christian or someone who is still working their identity out in Christ. They might struggle to walk with a pure heart because they can easily fall into the trap of agreeing with all the things they're hearing. It's even more difficult when all the compliments don't *seem* prideful because they are spiritual.

I realized I had a problem with this when the next person I prayed for was healed and I had a thought run through my head. *Yeah, I knew that was going to happen. God uses me.* I was instantly disgusted at how that sounded, and God rebuked me before I could even process it. He didn't have to say a word. I felt like a kid who had said something stupid at a dinner or in front of company. My dad only had to shoot me a look. That's all I needed.

Sometimes God's fathering is like that. If you're prideful, you'll get offended at God for correcting you. But if you love God and His Word, you'll find that His correction is not only necessary and for your benefit, but it's proof that He loves you. He corrects those He loves. When God corrected me, it stung at first, but He was keeping me from a prideful fall or from looking like a fool down the line.

Pride, unchecked, is one of the nastiest sins and creates the most damage to the person and anyone associated when the fall eventually happens. As the Scripture says, "Pride goes before destruction, and a haughty spirit before a fall" (Proverbs 16:18). I'm thankful that pride never manifested itself outwardly, but God knows the heart and the mind. This is terrifying to those who are in sin but comforting to those who love God. As His children, we want His correction. We want Him to search us and know us, to point out any wrong thinking within us long before we ever act on it.

God saved me so many times from making a fool of myself, and I continue to welcome His voice to keep me on the straight and narrow. Hearing His voice isn't just, "Pray for that person" or "That person has problems with their father, and I want to encourage them."

Everyone wants those words, but we should truly crave the words of correction and guidance. An orphan lives free of correction, but a disciplined child longs for it because they see the value in it.

God taught me these lessons early on as I walked with Him and pursued the kingdom. As the Scripture promises, "But seek first the kingdom of God and His righteousness, and all these things shall be added to you" (Matthew 6:33). Normal Christianity is seeking the kingdom of God and His righteousness. From that place, everything else will naturally follow.

As I talk about my walk with Christ and seeing the supernatural, I'd be remiss if I didn't share some of these pitfalls that God helped me avoid. I don't just want to be a man who encourages people to run after the gifts of the Spirit without teaching about the character and integrity of heart needed to go with it. Maybe you're like me and got radically set on fire for Jesus but didn't have a big community of Spirit-filled Christians to run with. You might struggle if you feel alone in that walk and feel as if you're one of the only people in your circle who is pursuing the supernatural.

I hope that as you read this, you find the desperation I felt to be fathered by God. I hope that you intentionally seek out a few people who are like-minded to build friendships with, like I did with Jacob. You need to be discipled, you need to be fathered, and you need to be sharpened by brothers and sisters around you who are burning just the same as you are. "As iron sharpens iron, so a man sharpens the countenance of his friend" (Proverbs 27:17).

Faith in Jesus

At this point in my walk, maybe six to eight months in, I felt like I was on a treadmill of learning, and God was constantly increasing the speed. I felt graced with the capacity to keep up, but only by leaning on Him. Imagine a bigger treadmill that could fit two people on it, one in front of the other. I felt as if Jesus was running and I was holding on to the back of His shirt. The only way I could keep up was by not letting go. As He increased in speed, my only job was to keep holding on. I want to present to you what the writer of Hebrews penned:

> Therefore we also, since we are surrounded by so great a cloud of witnesses, let us lay aside every weight, and the sin which so easily ensnares us, and let us run with endurance the race that is set before us, looking unto Jesus, the author and finisher of our faith.
>
> Hebrews 12:1–2

We are in a race, not a race to win salvation nor to earn the attention or affection of God. He has already shown us His love when He sent us His Son (Romans 5:8). To those of us who are born again, we have already received the free gift of salvation by grace through faith (Ephesians 2:8–9). Now we are on a narrow path, running for the victory, which is finishing this life with continued faith in God. And the writer of Hebrews tells us to run with endurance. Paul tells us to "run in such a way as to win a prize" (1 Corinthians 9:24, my paraphrase). In this race, your victory does not make you holy or righteous. We are made holy and righteous by the sacrifice of Jesus Christ (Colossians 1:22). This race is a race of faith.

You run the race to win by having faith that doesn't fail. Life can bring us more than just curveballs; sometimes, it feels like a fast pitch to the face. The Bible promises that God is faithful to keep us who belong to Him. Jesus said, "My Father, who has given them to Me, is greater than all; and no one is able to snatch them out of My Father's hand" (John 10:29). *Your ability to run the race well and endure till the end is not based on your faith but on His faithfulness!* We have a part to play in that we must believe. But when your faith is weak, He is made strong. Having faith in God doesn't mean you have to feel like you're on a mountaintop, ready to take on the world for Jesus. Having faith that endures can look like facing a seemingly immovable mountain, feeling like all is lost and there's no hope, seeing tons of reasons why the mountain will never move, and declaring this:

God, I see this mountain, and I know you do too. Right now, I choose by faith to trust in you. When I have every reason in my flesh to doubt, to not believe, and to feel overwhelmed, I choose to believe in you. I choose by faith to put my hope and trust in you. I know you will see me through this. I love you. Help me to keep following and trusting in you. In Jesus's name. Amen.

That is faith! Faith isn't about feelings but is actually standing on truth even when it directly opposes your feelings. This is an incredibly important principle to live by, and we see it play out not just in our faith walk (believing in Jesus for our salvation and eternal life) but also in daily life. As I said, I felt as if I was on a treadmill, holding on to Jesus as He ran. This run we were on reminded me of my military training when I was on the path to becoming an army officer. I felt like I was in Holy Spirit boot camp. The expression "drinking from a firehose" came to mind, but I had been enjoying every second of it because I realized that I had been so thirsty for twenty-five years and never truly had drank from the living waters of Jesus. Now that I had tasted, I couldn't get enough. So I kept asking Him for more. "Show me more, Lord" became my daily prayer. I didn't want to miss out on anything Jesus had for me that I had missed out on for the first part of my life.

Signs That Make You Wonder

The longer I did this, the more normal I felt. Sure, compared to many other people around me, I felt weird, but when I was with Jesus or my friends who were burning for Him, I felt more alive than ever. I began to see that *this* was normal and that the way I had been living previously was not. I saw how I'd been programmed by my flesh and by the world, that is under demonic influence, to pursue the normal things of life, which were actually counter to the things of God. I saw how living "your best life" actually puts you in a position to dictate what is best and leaves God out of the picture entirely.

I began to say, "Lord, help me die so that you can live *your* life through me." This is the way. I saw that the more I stepped out in faith and the bigger risks I took, the less I cared about what people thought of me. I was more than willing to embarrass myself for the sake of showing Christ to the world. I thought about the nights I had spent partying downtown and how foolish I must have looked to God. Now, I delighted in looking like a fool to the world in order to follow the lead of my Father in heaven. This wonderful exchange took place in my heart and in my mind, and I never had to *try* to be holy or righteous. I never tried to do anything except seek God and find out His will. I didn't try to be anything except intentional about my time with Him.

The natural result of daily pursuing a relationship with Him was the renewing of my mind to love what He loved and to leave behind the cares and desires of the world as well as the opinions of man. I was filled with reckless abandonment of my ego or reputation. Only in this place of freedom can you truly walk with God in the manner He so desires. Only from this place of liberation from the fear of man can you live the normal Christian life.

I soon saw radical miracles that blew my mind. Once, I was driving in my Jeep after a day at the police academy near Seattle, and I asked God to take me somewhere. I began to pray in the Spirit, and a minute or so later, I saw a picture in my mind of this store called GameStop at the Tacoma Mall. I then, totally by faith, asked God what was going to happen there. I began the forty-five-minute drive to the mall and prayed in the

Spirit again. I then saw a wide-open vision of a crooked spine against a white background. A giant hand came from the side of the image and pushed the spine back into the correct shape and posture. I saw all of this with my eyes open while driving on the highway.

I believed that God was showing me that someone was going to be healed of a significant spinal issue at the mall. I quickly wrote this information on my phone and began to pray over this person by faith and thank God for what He was going to do and the healing that would take place. I also recorded a video where I said all of this beforehand so that when all this happened, I would have it documented. That way, there would be no doubt that it was God and not some coincidence.

It's important to understand, especially if you are new to all this, that I was driving to the mall in absolute faith. I didn't hear a voice, I didn't see a sign on the road, and the clouds didn't open with writing in the sky. All this stemmed from thoughts and images in my head. I didn't know if I was just imagining these things or if it was God, but I was willing to risk wasting my time by taking a chance that God was actually speaking to me. I didn't care about my time. I cared more about following God and trying to learn His voice, and I was willing to do anything to hear Him speak and to be used by Him. So I drove, praying for a person who may or may not exist about a possible condition in their back that may or may not exist at the Tacoma Mall where they may or may not be. Ha!

As I approached the mall, parked, and began to walk in, my heart was racing. I thanked God for being with me and walked toward GameStop from the west wing of the mall, because I felt like God told me to enter from there. I reached the point in the center of the mall where all four wings meet. GameStop was ahead to my right, and as I approached it, a man was leaning on a cane and walking with a severe limp. I thought, *Oh my gosh, this is him!* I walked up to him and said, "Sir, this is going to sound crazy, but do you have issues with your back?"

He looked at me and said, "Yes, why?" I pulled out the notes on my phone and showed him what I had written, including the time stamp that showed it was typed a half hour earlier. As I showed him this, the Lord began to speak to me in more detail. The thought "disc degeneration" came to my mind. I asked him if this was the issue he had, and he said yes. I told him God was going to heal him right there and asked if we could pray. He told me that we could, and he and his wife and family all joined hands with me as we prayed aloud in the center of the mall.

After the prayer, I asked him to test out his back. He picked up his cane and began to bend and move and then began to dance and hop around. God had miraculously healed this man of all pain and limitation. We were in awe of God and praised Him and gave Him glory right there in front of the Starbucks, with GameStop just beyond it. I took a video testimony of what happened and shared it on social media for the world to see all that God had done.[1]

Over the next few months, I would experience countless encounters like this one, where I believed I heard the Lord and went in faith and saw the power of His healing hands move over those I would meet. I traveled to random places at the voice of the Lord to give words of knowledge and encouragement and prophesy over total strangers that God divinely chose for me to encounter. I also experienced my fair share of trips to random places where I met no one. I drove to places I believed I heard in prayer or saw in my mind after asking God, only to find I was alone when I got there with not a soul in sight. This is the faith journey with God.

Each time I found myself alone or in places where I didn't find the person I believed I saw in my mind, I laughed and prayed. I'd thank God that I was still learning His voice, and I thanked Him for the heart He put in me to keep pursuing Him, never being discouraged by missing it. The journey of hearing God has had plenty of misses and successes, but the journey isn't measured that way. God is looking for your faith and obedience.

When you think you hear God and act upon it, He is pleased with your faith. Whether the thing comes to pass or not, it makes no difference in the grand scheme of eternity. What matters is, can God trust you to move when you believe He's spoken? I want it to be said about me that I was a wild follower of His voice, even if it made me look foolish. I'd wasted plenty of my time playing in the devil's territory and doing his will. I was happy to waste my time running around my city, believing I heard God's voice.

Your Next Leap of Faith

I hope the following radical true story of faith will absolutely supercharge yours. I do not say that lightly. I shared this story on my YouTube channel (@shanewinnings), and it has over seven million views, and for good reason. This is a wild, challenging, inspiring short story of someone who took a leap of faith, and it changed two lives for eternity.

A woman was at a prayer meeting and desired to give more to God. She was hungry for more, so she said this to Him, "God, whatever you ask me to do for the next thirty days, I will do it. I don't care how ridiculous it is, if I believe it is from you, I'll do it." What a simple prayer that has the power to flip your world upside down. Now, I know this goes without saying, but I always say it: God will not ask you to do anything that is illegal, immoral, or unethical. For anything else, you simply run the risk of looking foolish.

So she prayed this and, shortly after, left the meeting to drive home. On her drive home, she found herself at a red light and looked over at a 7-Eleven convenience store. She immediately saw a picture in her mind of herself standing on her head in the middle of the store. She did what most of us do at a random, silly thought: shook her head and looked back at the road, waiting for the green light. A thought popped in her mind. *I thought you said you'd do anything.*

She instantly recognized that God was speaking—it wasn't just her crazy idea. She knew she had to go, and so she turned into the parking lot, walked inside, and stood on her head. Suddenly, an employee came out of the back room and began screaming and crying. The woman got up from the ground and said, "What? What's wrong?"

The employee said, "I was just in the back room praying, and I told God, 'God, I need to know if you're real. Send someone in here to stand on their head, or I'm going to kill myself after work tonight.'" Both women cried, and the woman from the prayer group led the employee to the Lord. Her life was saved and forever changed. Hallelujah!

Every time I share this story, I feel the presence of the Lord come over me. This powerful story shows the simplicity of following the voice of God and how it can flip your life and the lives of others upside down. Do you want this? Both women were changed forever, and that thirty-day commitment the woman gave to God turned into a lifetime commitment.

God is faithful and wants to use you to change the world around you. He wants to use you to bring hope, encouragement, and life to those who are hurting, lost, and broken. He wants to use you to bring the gospel to them. This miracle of a woman on her head was just a means to share the gospel. It was a door to evangelism that God didn't just open but kicked off its hinges. When you follow God, you'll see Him open doors to the hearts and minds of the most closed off and unsuspecting people. All it takes is your obedience and willingness.

I want to challenge you to take the same leap of faith this woman did. Tell God, as sincerely as you can, that you want to know Him more, follow His lead, and be used by Him just like He used that woman in the story. Then commit to being obedient when He speaks.

Pause and Pray

Let's capitalize on this moment right now by praying. Even after typing this, I sense a grace for God to multiply this and do it again. Whenever you hear a testimony that provokes you to see the greater things of God, whether in your own mind, heart, and life, or greater manifestations of His glory, an invitation on the back end says, "Lord, do that in me. Do it again, God."

We just read about three different areas in a fun and stretching season I stepped into when I was first born again. I talked about walking in integrity and purity of heart and mind, about staying in faith and running the race to win, and about normal Christianity. Reflect on those areas and begin to determine in your heart what you want to receive from them. Are you looking to go deeper in your walk with God, allowing Him to actually father you and speak to the areas of your life that He wants to purify? Do you desire to run hard and finish this race of faith, having run with endurance? Do you deeply desire to walk in the supernatural as if it were as normal as going to buy groceries?

The invitation has been extended to you. The grace to receive it in your own life is here. Pray with me, but also bring forth another prayer when we finish, one from the very depths of your being. Be completely honest with God about what you want and ask Him to begin to form and mold you to walk it out. He is faithful to do it.

Father, I thank you in the name of Jesus for loving me. I thank you for your faithfulness to keep me on the narrow path. You are a perfect father, and I'm asking you right now to treat me as a child. Correct me, discipline me, rebuke me, chasten me, and lead and guide me as a good father does. I don't want to be a lord unto myself. I don't want to make my own decisions in the way that I think is right. I want to be led by you. I want to follow your voice. I'm asking you to speak to the depths of my soul, search my heart, examine my mind, and reveal any way within me that isn't like you. Thank you that you'll do it with love and for the purpose of refining me to live more like Jesus. I want to walk with the Holy Spirit, step by step. I want to see miracles. I want to hear your voice for others and give words of knowledge and prophecy. I want to be used by you in greater ways than I've even read about or heard about. You have my yes. Above all, teach me purity of heart and mind. I want to be an obedient child who does everything out of love and nothing out of selfish ambition. I love you, God. Thanks for loving me first. In the name of your Son, Jesus Christ, I pray, Amen.

7

Wielding Your Spiritual Sword

Did you know that God has given you a spiritual sword? The most powerful weapon we have is the Word. Revelation 19 even describes Jesus as returning with a sword coming from His mouth. I had to learn how to mold my life around the Word and wield it just like a solider would wield his weapon. I continued sharing the gospel everywhere I went, seeing many miracles and hearts turning to God.

After a year or so of walking with God, I had already seen the deaf, blind, mute, crippled, cancer-stricken, and all kinds of people who were afflicted with infirmities totally healed by God. In late 2016, I went on a mission trip to Cambodia and Thailand and saw the same type of miracles I saw in the Tacoma Mall. The lie of "you have to go on a mission trip to see a miracle" was falling flat.

People don't see miracles in America because we don't pray for them. All of my friends who pray for the sick see miracles, and my friends who don't, see nothing. People on mission trips feel more emboldened to share their faith for a number of reasons, mostly because they might never see these people again and don't have to worry about their reputation. However, how many people do you know who will ask to pray for a co-worker at the water cooler? Sadly, a lot more is at stake because we've put our stake in our reputations instead of putting our stake in the finished work of Christ. If we really believed the gospel and we truly knew that Christ was a healer, we would pray for everyone without care of our reputation among man. We must break off this mentality of the cares of this world and the fear of man if we are going to live a life of faith. You will never take your next leap of faith if you are worried about what the crowd might say.

I'd constantly put myself in situations where I would look totally foolish. I didn't do this to *be* a fool but to intentionally kill my flesh and any desires to maintain a status among men. My friends back in Washington will tell you I was pretty good at embarrassing myself for Christ. When I was a new believer, I was always trying to get a word of knowledge for our server, often being wrong. "Excuse me, is your birthday August 7?" I'd ask.

"No, why?" they'd respond.

"Oh, I was just asking God when your birthday was, and I thought I heard that." These were normal interactions for me. I was so desperate to hear God's voice and share it with the rest of the world and, at the same time, desperate to destroy the fear of man in my life, that I took these big risks where either I was right or wrong. There's no wiggling out of guessing someone's birthday wrong.

I could ask safe and more generalized questions, even opening a door for me to make some swirly spiritual connection and save some face. No, I didn't want that. Maybe it was the military side of me, but I wanted to go for it. At times, I did hear God correctly, which was absolutely incredible. Our server would feel so touched and known, and my friends and I would minister to them with accuracy and such love that they would often cry. Even in the many times that I missed it, because love was the goal and not getting a word right, they felt encouraged that I would even ask God about them. Usually, they let me pray for them before the night was over.

My goal was never to be right—it was to love. My goal was to lay my hands on every person I could and pray for them to encounter and know the one true God. The more I did this, the less I began to care about myself in regard to reputation or opinions of others. It was a much-needed shedding of any pride or ego that tried to hide in me. After a year and a half of living this way, I felt absolutely free from man, even preaching out in the open on planes, buses, and in other public places.

On one occasion, I believed I heard God, and it was a word I didn't want to give. I was on vacation in Viera, Florida, where I grew up, visiting my parents in the summer of 2017 for a few weeks. I'd been born again for about a year and a half, and had been a police officer for around the same length of time. Since then, I had been working fifty to sixty hours a week, if not more, and working as much overtime as possible to pay off debt and save up some money so that I'd be prepared for marriage one day when I met the right girl. I had saved up six weeks of time off, so I spent three weeks in Tacoma and the second three weeks in Florida. I will say this, there is nothing like a staycation followed by a trip somewhere else. I had never felt so refreshed in my life.

One afternoon, I went to Starbucks to read my Bible like I had done every day on vacation. As I was standing in line, I saw this man in front of me, looking intently toward the back corner of the coffee shop. I looked over to see what he was looking at, and it was a girl who was dressed immodestly, to say the least. I saw a wedding ring on this man's finger, and as I shook my head and looked back toward the barista, I had an open vision for the first time in my life.

I saw a screen where the menu should be, and a movie began playing on it. I was wide awake and fully aware of my surroundings. It was bizarre. On the screen, this man was pulling up to a motel in a vehicle, getting out, and walking up to the second floor, where he met a woman. They embraced and then went inside one of the rooms. I instantly felt the spirit of adultery and lust come over me, and I could have vomited and cried at the same time. I knew that this woman was not his wife. The screen disappeared, and the menu was back in its place.

I knew that I was to speak with this man about the vision I'd had, but I was incredibly terrified. What if I were wrong? What if I had imagined this whole thing? What if this vision I had was simply my imagination running wild, based on my observation of him staring at the inappropriately dressed girl? All these questions ran through my mind in about two seconds. I had no answers to them, but I did know God. Often, I have questions that don't have answers, but I do know God. Relationship with Him is so important because you realize that you don't need answers, you just need Him.

As I stood in line, I realized that I could either ignore this vision and try to go on with my life, or I could take a risk and act in faith, believing it was God and that something miraculous was about to happen. I committed in my heart to talking with this man, asked God to fill me with strength and courage, and tapped the man on the shoulder.

"Excuse me, sir. I really need to speak with you in private. Can we go outside?" I asked.

"Um, okay," he responded. Both of us walked outside, away from the crowd of people nearby. My heart was racing as I began to tell him of the vision I had. As I was sharing the vision, I began to download more information about this man's life. He struggled with pornography, and this issue of lust affected his relationship with his son. I shared these words with him as well. I ended by saying this, "God showed me all of this because He loves marriage, and He loves your marriage. He wants to save it, and He sent me to tell you, 'Don't do it.'"

The man looked as if he had been caught red-handed. Conviction often feels that way. We have a Father who confronts us about things that we never even get the chance to do because He cares too much about us. This man looked like I had just shown up that night to the motel room in a priest's robe and caught him in the act. I once again said, "Please don't do it."

He said, "Okay" and left. I never saw him again, but I believe a life and a marriage were saved that day. God doesn't share information for no reason. God tells us things because He wants to act on them. God would not let that man act however he wanted without being first confronted with the voice of the Father. That is the mercy of God, to visit a man in a Starbucks and try to intervene on a potentially life-changing and destructive decision.

What choice the man made, I do not know. What I do know is that from that moment, he either had to harden himself to God completely to do what he wanted or repent and go home. The Spirit of God was so heavy in that parking lot and the conviction was so intense, that I believe he chose the latter, and I prayed as I left that he did.

After this wild encounter, I drove to a local church parking lot and went live on Facebook. I shared what happened for about six minutes and that was that. I was hanging out with one of my best friends, playing drums while he played guitar, and my phone was buzzing non-stop. I looked and saw that my video was beginning to go viral with a few thousand views within an hour or so. On Facebook, this was a big deal, especially since I had a little more than a thousand friends and averaged seventy to a hundred likes on a post. A few hours later, it was at more than ten thousand views.

The next morning, it was double that, eventually reaching nearly fifty thousand views. Each time I would refresh the Facebook app, a new thumbnail picture of someone popped up, and the notification said, "John Smith and fifty other people liked your video." One time, after refreshing, it said, "Jessica Oliver and forty-nine other people liked your video." I saw the little picture of Jessica and thought, *That has got to be the most beautiful girl I've ever seen!*

I clicked on her profile to see what she was all about. I was actually looking for a reason to forget about her entirely. I'd dated enough girls in the world and in the church and had seen the trend that always led to a horrible relationship. I was tired of superficial Christianity or a form of Christianity that looked good but had no power. I was tired of seeing girls posting pictures of themselves in their bikinis with Bible verses in the caption. I had dated enough girls like that and knew that another relationship would end the same as it always did. No, I wanted depth. I wanted Jesus. I wanted a girl who loved God more than I did. I wanted a girl who valued purity and honor, who had integrity, and who didn't ride the fence between worldly and righteous living.

So I scoured Jessica's page, looking for reasons to move on. I looked for a reason to end it before it ever started. To my pleasant surprise, the more I looked, the more I was convinced she actually loved Jesus. Every picture was beyond modest. The posts she made about

Christ actually had depth, and I felt like she really knew Him. I went from being afraid that she would mess up my relationship with Jesus to believing that she might actually make it stronger. I had seen all I needed to see and decided to send her a message. Little did I know that saying "Hey!" would turn into the life I have now.

This isn't just a story for you to read, but a testimony for you to grab on to and say, "God, do it in me." Whenever you hear a testimony, it releases faith for God to do it again. You might be desperately desiring to be used by God; believe that He will use you and that He wants to use you. You might be longing for companionship in a spouse and dream of building a family that serves the Lord together. Trust in God and His timing. This story is much more than a story, but a testimony of how God moved upon small acts of obedience that led to bigger ones. As you're reading this, let faith arise in your heart for God to do it again, in you.

Bearing Each Other's Burdens

After a year of long-distance dating, Jessica and I got married, and she moved from Tennessee to Washington. We bought a house together and stepped into the next phase of life as a married couple. After five years of marriage, I will tell you that the honeymoon phase can be a lifestyle. In this book about faith, I want you to know that it is completely possible to live in a state of bliss in your marriage. This all depends on marrying the right person as well as being filled by God every single day so that you have something to give your spouse instead of waking up with something to need or expect from them. Unmet expectations cause the biggest issues in marriage, but Jessica and I have been blessed to live without expecting anything from each other.

This entire topic is another book that might be in the works, but I'll just tell you that marriage can be amazing. Ours has gotten better every day since we met with no sign of slowing down.

Part of our new life together was bearing each other's burdens. Jessica was diagnosed with epilepsy at a young age and had experienced seizures here and there. I have never had to release control as much as I have being married to Jessica because the truth is that I cannot control her health. I have prayed for her to be healed countless times, and we have seen God move in incredible ways, but we have yet to see her full deliverance. In this waiting, I have learned to trust God.

I want to fix everything, which can be a great quality, until the want becomes a need. You know as well as I do that there is nothing worse than needing something that you can't have. We tend to believe the lie that we need things other than Jesus. I struggled in some seasons of our marriage with feeling out of control in regard to Jessica's health and praying from a place of control, which is usually rooted in some sort of fear. God had to deliver me of fear. I wasn't even afraid that Jessica would die or that something specific would happen to her, but I was afraid of not being in control and of being able to stop what was happening to my wife. Praise God for His perfect fathering, because He patiently led me through the process of dying to my need to have circumstances go my way and to learn to trust Him in the waiting.

Jessica felt the Lord say that it was time to wean off her medication because of the horrible side effects, including potential fertility issues. At this point, we really wanted to be parents and wanted to make sure Jessica was off medicine for a while before we tried. In faith, Jessica slowly came off her prescriptions until, one day, she was completely off them. She was doing great, and she didn't have many issues until one night. We were watching a movie at home, and all of a sudden, the temperature drastically plummeted in the room. Jessica said, "Something's not right" and then instantly went into a seizure.

It felt as if a demon had walked right into our room and touched her. I began to pray and command it to stop, and after a short time, she came out of it. That night, we cried and prayed together and listened to worship as we got our bearings. This was the first time this had happened in the three years that we had been together, and the way it happened felt demonic. As we took the next few days to process this and pray, one morning, the Lord spoke to me. "Jessica is thinking she made a mistake getting off the medicine, but tell her to watch what I'm about to do."

I leaned out of the bathroom where I was getting ready for the day and said, "Hey, do you think you made a mistake going off your meds?"

She responded, "Yeah, I do."

I said, "Well, God just told me that, and He said to watch what He was about to do." We both got excited as our faith began to rise. What God was about to do was a mighty work in both of our lives in ways we'd never expected.

Right now, you might be walking through a season of uncertainty and doubt. Rest assured that God is not far from you and that you were created to overcome this. It would be wrong of me to tell you what to do in this season of your life, because I don't know where you're at, and to simply apply what Jessica and I walked through to your situation would not be wise. The take-away from this is to trust in God and continue to build your relationship with Him. Everything Jess and I did was out of obedience, believing we were hearing God's voice and then acting on it.

For your situation, do the same. Ask God what to do, then take a leap of faith and do it. Faith is not a copy-and-paste method of living but a choice we make based on a relationship that we have. Let this encourage you to go deeper in your walk with Jesus, because with Him, nothing is impossible.

A Gift, a Brush with Death, and a Ministry

A few days after the demonic attack, Jessica began to get the urge to draw. She had doodled here and there but had never had any formal art training except the one class in school that we all took growing up. She picked up a pencil and drew a self-portrait that was pretty decent. She then drew a picture of Jesus as depicted by

Akiane Kramarik. This picture was incredibly close to the original, and at that moment, Jessica and I began to realize that something was happening with her and this new drawing desire. She began to draw more portraits, and each one became more and more realistic until her fourth or fifth one looked like a black-and-white photo.

She did this with no training in the span of a few months. We knew that God was speaking about the attack that night, and we felt like He said, "The enemy tried to take something from you, but I'm giving you a gift." Jessica went from doodling to doing portraits for clients and selling them for more than a thousand dollars. This was a true miracle, a blessing to our family, and a kick to the teeth of the enemy who thought he'd come in and robbed us of our peace and joy.

I'm so thankful that God is rich in mercy, because the enemy has none. In the same season that Jessica was attacked demonically, we found mold in our kitchen floors and had to rip out our entire kitchen: cabinets, floors, and even the subfloor. Yes, I mean every single bit of it. We went through a three- to four-month battle with our insurance company regarding the repairs.

To make a long story short, the quote to fix everything was nearly forty thousand dollars, and the insurance company wanted to pay us ten thousand dollars. As we went back and forth on the phone for months and months, we had no kitchen. It was an empty room with bare walls, some of which were ripped out, and plywood floors. As if this demonic encounter weren't enough, circumstances at my job decided to ramp up one night as well.

I was doing a routine patrol drinking my one-dollar drink from Dutch Bros. (Shout-out to Dutch Bros in Federal Way, Washington, for your incredible support of police.) A call came in about a recently stolen RV. My partner, Anders, and I, in separate vehicles, drove toward the area and began to check for the RV. Within a few minutes, Anders had located it, and I pulled in behind him. We followed the RV for a minute or two as it was confirmed stolen. Anders and I had conducted stops on probably hundreds of stolen cars in our time at the department, and while there is always a very real element of danger, we were very familiar and comfortable with these types of situations. Suspects in stolen cars will either pull over (extremely rare) or run (extremely common). We had been in too many pursuits to count and were prepared for this to head that direction as well.

We began calling out the streets in the area to get spike strips set up so that if this person did try to flee, we'd be able to stop them. As Anders and I were doing this, we followed the RV at normal speeds. You don't want to turn on your lights and siren before everything is set up; otherwise, they'll take off, and you'll be unprepared, as will the rest of your squad. We were talking over the radio, getting our squad mates into position, when the suspect in the RV began to pull off the road and slam on the brakes, bringing the vehicle to a complete stop. With a sudden maneuver like this, I was expecting the driver to jump out and either run or start shooting.

Anders and I both pulled off to the side of the RV and prepared to exit our vehicles, weapons drawn, when the suspect began driving again. This happened three or four times, and I began to get anxious as to what would happen. The problem with this is that action always beats reaction. With the suspect swerving and stopping this fast, it was impossible for me to follow, stop, get out, and engage fast enough should they decide to start shooting.

I started driving with my gun drawn and pointed up toward the RV when the vehicle did the same maneuver again, this time stopping for an extra few seconds. As a cop, you never want to be caught in your car. The windshield will not provide protection from gunfire, and you can't move if you're in a seat. I threw open my door and jumped out, as did Anders, who was slightly ahead of me and off to the left.

As per standard procedure, I began to issue verbal commands to the driver to turn off the RV and exit the vehicle with their hands up. The next thing I know, the reverse lights came on, and the RV was barreling toward me. I made a split decision to try to run for a nearby ditch, as my other option was to get back inside my vehicle and take the hit, potentially pinning me in and leaving me defenseless and immobile. As I began to run, the RV scraped against Anders's car as he dove into the ditch. I ran as fast as I could when suddenly a vehicle hit me in the hip, which sent me flying more than thirty feet.

I looked up from the ground as the RV came toward me, pushing my police vehicle with it. The suspect hadn't just hit my vehicle but was now trying to run me over. I quickly propped my foot up on the door frame of my police vehicle and allowed it to push me as I skidded along the road on my back. I was either unharmed, full of adrenaline, or both, but managed to jump up and ran to get an angle to shoot the driver. As I raised my firearm, the suspect threw the RV into gear and sped off down the street and around a corner. Most of my equipment had fallen out of my police belt, including my radio.

I tried to relay what had happened to my squad mates as Anders ran toward me to make sure I was okay. A quick trip to the ER and some X-rays showed that nothing was broken, and I went home a few hours later with nothing more than some scrapes on my knees and arms and a gnarly bruise on my hip. Although I had survived this incident, it felt like another blow from the enemy in this spiritual war that Jessica and I were knee-deep in. As I flew through the air that night, I thought, *Is this really how I'm going to die, Lord?*

I'm so thankful He said, "No, it's not."

Shortly after this incident, the pandemic of 2020 followed. As a cop, I still went to work at night, and not much changed for us other than not being able to go out to eat. As we were navigating this season in a very locked-down city, Jessica encountered God dramatically. While I was at work one night, she sent me a video message, bawling her eyes out as she told me that God said, "Ministry is just around the corner."

Little did I know that two weeks later, the Minneapolis incident with George Floyd would occur. I found myself fundraising to fly out and evangelize that area as they desperately needed the gospel. Looting and rioting were taking over the streets, and I felt a pull to bring the presence of God into that place. I miraculously raised a thousand dollars in a few hours through a simple Facebook post, and a few days later, I was on a plane to Minnesota. This trip would catapult me into the next phase of my life and take my ministry from the streets to the digital space. Jessica and I were beginning to see God's redemptive plan in the midst of our trials.

Maybe you are in a season of trials and warfare, and you haven't seen the redemption yet. Stay faithful. I have to share all these things with you so that you understand why I am the way that I am. If you've seen me preach, it's probably been about dying to self and understanding your correct identity in Christ so that you can live a life of faith. If you didn't know that I'd ever gone through anything difficult, you could easily sit through one of my messages and say, "Well, that's easy for you to say" without having any knowledge of what I've walked through.

Some of the most passionate preachers I know are not preaching a sermon they heard somewhere. They are preaching the testimony of God in their lives. They are preaching the Word of God that came alive during a season (or seasons) of absolute crushing. My passion and conviction come from a firsthand account as the God of the Bible revealed Himself to me in real time. The Word I've been studying and reading, the God I've been praying to and worshiping became more than someone who sits up in heaven. I've seen God as Emmanuel, God *with* me. I've seen Jehovah Rapha, the God who heals.

I want to encourage you as you read to look at the fires you're walking through and begin to see how God is in them with you. Look back or look at your current situation and find the workings of God in the midst of the trial. If you can't seem to find Him yet, release faith and gratitude by speaking this over your life: "God, I thank you that it isn't any worse." What marks a believer in seasons of trial is the perspective we carry. The Bible says we are not without hope like those who don't even know God. (See 1 Thessalonians 4:13.)

Becoming a TikTok Preacher

My trip to the heart of the Black Lives Matter movement was recorded on video, and the footage would spark a series of online interviews, social media posts, and opportunities to share the gospel on various podcasts. As I started to navigate this online presence, some of my friends were making Christian content on an app called TikTok. I had only heard about it at work and chalked it up to be another teen app like Snapchat used for inappropriate reasons. Jacob actually was the first person I knew who used it, and to be honest, I initially thought it was totally ridiculous, but I was thankful for a friend like him who would stop at nothing to get the gospel out. It also helped that he told me he wasn't dancing in the videos. Ha-ha!

Even so, I wasn't convinced to join and definitely didn't want another app to waste my time on, as I knew

I was already spending too much time scrolling on the ones I had. A few months went by, and Jacob's brother, Jonah, started preaching on TikTok as well. In just over a month, he gained forty thousand followers. I was blown away by the amount of people he was reaching, and I knew instantly that I had to do it too. I thought, *I could be reaching tens of thousands with my preaching*. I was already posting little things on Instagram, but my content would get a few hundred views at best. I created an account and began posting videos. I saw that you needed one thousand followers to be able to stream live, and that became my goal. I just wanted a thousand followers so that I could preach the gospel once a week, live, and reach people for Jesus.

I gained those thousand followers within a week or so and began preaching every Monday night at what I called TikTok Church. Within a few weeks, a video went viral, amassing over three hundred and fifty thousand views, and I gained twenty thousand followers. I kept telling Jessica, "You'll never believe this. I just gained another thousand followers!" Before long, it was too much to keep up with, and I had to turn off notifications on the app. I went from responding to every single comment and DM to not being able to respond fast enough because more would come in. Within a few months, I was over three hundred thousand followers and had several viral videos with millions of views each. I officially had an online ministry, with literally thousands of people watching me preach live every Monday night.

During these lives, I would preach for about thirty to forty-five minutes, sometimes an hour, and then pray for the sick. During this time of prayer, I'd go after words of knowledge and prophecy. Through this working of the Holy Spirit, my live audience doubled every week for a few months. The last live session I did on TikTok had more than nine thousand people come through in the ninety-minute meeting.

One night in particular marked me forever. Earlier in the day, I was praying with Jessica as we tried to do together. The Lord spoke, "Brain issue." I immediately thought of live church, which was a few hours later, and believed that God was giving me a word of knowledge. After preaching, I began to minister and pray for the sick. I asked if anyone had a brain issue. One woman commented, "I have an aneurysm in my brain, and it has a daughter aneurysm growing on it." I asked everyone to reach their hand toward the screen as I prayed a simple prayer, commanding her brain to be healed and the aneurysm to go. The woman commented shortly after the prayer and testified that she had been experiencing a constant, unceasing headache for thirty days straight, twenty-four hours a day, and that it instantly stopped when I prayed. Everyone in the comments section was going wild, praising God and giving Him glory.

But it didn't stop there. The woman told me that she had an MRI coming up in a few days and that she would share the results with me after she got them. Later that week, I had a DM on Instagram from her with a voice message stating she had gotten her brain scan and *the aneurysm was gone!* She told me that the doctor was baffled because her aneurysm was so large that it was at risk of rupturing, as well as the fact that it had a secondary aneurysm growing on it. The best-case scenario, which in itself would be a miracle, would be that both of them shrank over the course of a year or so. According to the doctor, it was unheard of that this thing would completely disappear in under a month. To God be the glory!

The woman shared her testimony in a video, and I reposted it, gaining tens of thousands of views and attracting more and more people to the live stream on Monday nights.

This was just one of many radical testimonies that happened through online preaching. By the end of 2020, I was approaching half a million followers and had reached more than sixty million people for the gospel in just six months. This explosion of growth would lead me to my next leap of faith—walking away from my six-figure job into mission work with no guaranteed paycheck.

Some of you might read this and disqualify yourself from doing anything like this. While we are not all called to be evangelists and preachers (there are four other offices in the fivefold ministry), I want to make sure that you are not motivated by fear but led by the voice of God. You could easily read what I've done and say, "Well, that was for him, not me. I'm just a so-and-so." No, my friend. Do not ever disqualify who God has called qualified. Do not ever partner with the voice of the enemy who will talk down to you and discourage you from being bold and moving in faith.

The same door of opportunity to reach the nation and world for Jesus stands before you as it stood before me and the multitudes of preachers who have gone before us. The question today is, will you take the first step and open it?

Your Next Leap of Faith

Life happens fast, and it happens to all of us. Reading a chapter like this can cause you to go into a place of introspection. I pray that something I said spoke to you in some capacity: Jessica's health, my near-death experience, the hardships of the pandemic, the rioting and looting during the "summer of love," as the media called it, or even being a spectator to these types of situations and feeling the heaviness of it all. The wonderful thing about faith is that it isn't based on your age, experience, feelings, or anything else. As we know, Hebrews defines it as believing in something you can't see.

In those trials that Jessica and I went through, individually and as a married couple, there were plenty of times when we didn't see God moving. We had plenty of times to doubt, to be offended at God, to let hurt creep in. By faith, we chose none of those things. Why would we doubt? We aren't alive for today, and we aren't alive for ourselves—we are living for God and for eternity. We wouldn't dare let a temporal inconvenience speak louder than truth. Why would we be offended or hurt? Because God didn't answer our prayers in the timely manner or method that we'd hoped for? No, because we trust God and we submit to Him as our perfect Father. We also yield to His lordship and believe the Scripture that says His ways are higher than ours (Isaiah 55:9).

For your next leap of faith, I want to challenge you to confront a mountain in your life that you may be ignoring or allowing to be bigger than God. Maybe you haven't addressed a certain fear because it seems huge and you don't see how it could break. Maybe you have a certain mindset that limits God, but it's all you've ever known and you're afraid of what life might look like if you allowed Him to come in and blow it up. Maybe you're facing similar situations to what Jessica and I did, and you're just hanging on day by day.

I want to challenge you to do more than just survive your battle. You were not created to merely get through life, but to thrive in Christ. Thriving doesn't always mean perfect health and sunny skies, but it does mean walking in peace and joy and not letting anything matter more than what matters most. This leap of faith isn't attractive, but it's necessary. Right now, I'm asking you to confront the hard things in life and go at them with a godly perspective. You will always overcome because He is the Overcomer and He lives in you. It's time to face your fears and tell them how big your God is.

Pause and Pray

I don't know how this chapter was for you, but it was heavy for me. Even though a few years have passed, it's wild to put myself back in those places and remember what we went through. Some of those times were very dark, but Christ always came in and lit up our world. I want to stop and pray for you to see the light in your world. I've found that sometimes a demonic cloud tries to drown out the light, and sometimes it's a self-imposed cloud, caused by a wrong perspective. Too many moments of being in my feelings instead of in truth brought a cloud over my life, but I'm here to tell you that it doesn't have to keep happening! The truth will set you free, and even though the trials will come and go, your peace and joy don't have to. Let's pray and give God the chance to step into our mess and bring His light.

Father, I thank you in the name of Jesus for loving me. Thank you that you see me. Your Word says that you know every hair on my head. You know my thoughts. You know a word before it reaches my tongue. God, thank you for being a present Father who sees me. Today, I give you permission to come in and light up any dark areas I'm living in. Correct any wrong ways of thinking. Deliver

134

me of any perspectives I have that aren't yours. I yield to you and your ways. God, help me have faith. Regardless of the trials I'm facing, I know that with you, I will always overcome. You haven't left me or forsaken me. You haven't forgotten or abandoned me. You see me, and you're working all things out for my good. Help me trust in you even when I can't see what you're doing. I love you, and I honor you. Your ways are higher than mine. I pray this in Jesus's name. Amen.

8

Receiving a Vision from the Lord and Risking Everything to Follow Jesus

What happens when you have received a word from God but don't fully understand it? That's where I found myself during this season of preaching on TikTok. In the natural, my rapidly expanding online presence could turn into some form of full-time ministry, but I didn't know how that would actually happen. I told the Lord that I would stay faithful in this online ministry, but I was also asking Him to show me a peek of what was to come around the corner. In this season, I became part of an online collaboration called the Jesus Clubs and began preaching on their weekly Zoom Bible studies and posting content on their page.

This turned into a weekend visit to their parent organization (One Voice Student Missions) headquarters in Allen, Texas. As I headed home on May 1, 2021, on a red-eye flight after that weekend, I was extremely anxious. In general, I am not an anxious person and am very used to operating under immense amounts of stress, so I knew that something more was going on. I began to pray and ask God what was happening to me. I felt no peace and couldn't even quiet my mind to focus any of my prayers. Whenever I get in places like this, I pray in tongues. The Bible says that at times, we won't even be able to put our feelings into words.

> Likewise the Spirit also helps in our weaknesses. For we do not know what we should pray for as we ought, but the Spirit Himself makes intercession for us with groanings which cannot be uttered.
>
> Romans 8:26

After about two minutes of praying in the Spirit, I had a vision of myself in Texas with the team I had just visited, and I instantly began weeping uncontrollably. I then had a thought, which I know was God speaking to me. *You have to do this.*

I asked God, "When?" And another thought came to me. *You'll never work another shift as a police officer.* I jumped on my phone and looked at my vacation days in my leave bank. I had three weeks of paid time off stored up.

I texted Jess and told her what had happened, to which she responded, "I knew something like this would happen." We both committed to praying to hear God speak to us for confirmation the next day, and we both felt overwhelming peace about this decision.

I called my boss and told him that I was putting in my notice and that I would not be working another shift because God had called me to be a missionary. He and the rest of my guys at work said they were not surprised and that this lifestyle seemed like the perfect fit for me. I was overjoyed at the thought of stepping into full-time ministry, but working through the discomfort of having to do so by living off donor support. My police job paid well, and after five years there and all the overtime I was working, I was easily making over one hundred thousand dollars a year with great benefits and time off. Stepping away from that and the security of a large paycheck every two weeks into the unknown was terrifying and thrilling at the same time. I knew that God would provide, but the how was still yet to be seen.

In moments like this, you see where you truly are in your walk with Jesus. It's easy to preach about faith and even easier to encourage others to step out in obedience. But at the moment when your career, your income, your security is tested, you find out what you truly believe. I can say this with confidence: It's only because of the hours and hours of time in the secret place with Jesus that I could make this decision without fear. This was not a difficult decision for us, not because we had everything figured out—far from it! It wasn't easy because we had all of our finances in order; we didn't have a single donor when I quit my job. It was easy because we *knew* that God was God and that He would provide for us because we believed He had called us to do this. A tried-and-true principle in the Bible is that if God calls you to it, He will provide for you to do it.

Within nineteen days of hearing God speak that word to me on my flight, I had quit my career. We had also sold our home, built up a team of donor support, and moved to Texas. Less than three weeks after hearing God, we were in our new home, and I was serving as a missionary.

Again, this isn't a method that can be replicated in your life to see if it works for you. This is the result of being obedient to the Lord and moving on His timeline. Many told us that it could take six to twelve months to be fully funded with enough income to support our family and that some never get fully funded. God did it for our family in fourteen days. In just two weeks, we had enough people step up and say that they would sponsor our family monthly so that we could step into full-time ministry and ensure that all our bills were paid. This was extremely rare for most of my friends in mission work.

I want to take this opportunity to thank every person who supports my family and the ministry I've been entrusted with. From family and friends to followers on social media, we have a solid team of donors who keep us afloat and help us put on incredible events, travel the country, preach, make tons of online content for YouTube and Instagram, run a podcast, and even sit down to type out this book. None of this would be possible if it weren't for you. Thank you! Life happens, and supporters come and go all the time due to financial situations. If you are reading this and want to join our team of donors, you can go to shanewinnings.com and click "give" at the top right hand of the screen. We'd be honored to have you support us and the ministry and would also love to see you on the monthly private Zoom calls that are only for donors. Thank you for giving if you feel led by the Lord to do so.

I want to take a moment and empower some of you who may feel called into mission work. If God is truly calling you to go, He will make a way. My story is not a one-off. So many missionaries around the world have forsaken the American dream and the 401(k) and benefits to serve God. Some feel called to the mountains, some feel called to the Pacific Islands, and some, like me, feel called to America. Wherever you are called, know that God will prepare a place for you.

Overcoming the Fear of Man in the Face of Adversity

After a few months of preaching on TikTok, I began to get the urge to lead gospel gatherings around my city. I was seeing real hunger for Jesus and for truth on social media, and it was stirring me to go into the city and take the power on social media to the streets. I was still evangelizing regularly, in parks and fields and out front of my local mall, but I wanted to do more than just show up and start preaching and praying. I wanted to organize intentional gatherings with no hype and no promise of anything except that God would be there. I wanted meetings where people only came because they wanted to hear the gospel or see God move in power.

I had watched Billy Graham crusades in my cop car on slow days and felt a burden to see these meetings of tens of thousands, even a hundred thousand, happen again. One day, I felt like God spoke something to me during prayer that would change everything. I was crying out for God to open doors of revival and I heard Him say, "Shane, no one is going to plan a revival and ask you to lead it. If you want to see it, you have to do it."

I left my time of prayer fired up and thought, *Okay, Lord, I'll plan a citywide revival!*

I then heard Him say, "I thought you wanted to reach the whole nation."

I was instantly convicted of how small I had dreamed. I thought, *I did . . . well, I do.* Right then, before I had time to talk myself out of it, I told Jess what I'd heard and shortly after made a TikTok video announcing that I was planning a nationwide gospel tour for the summer of 2021. This was completely in faith because we had no partnerships, no local church connections, no venues, no permits, no money, and all of this was happening eight months into the pandemic with no idea of what the next summer would look like. But I thought I had heard God, so in my mind I had no other option.

In the meantime, I couldn't wait for summer to arrive, so I began posting about where I'd be preaching and did mini tours around my county. I organized an event in North Tacoma at Vassault Park. I wanted to see if paid advertising was effective, so I bought two-weeks' worth of focused social media ads and made digital flyers and even videos promoting the event. The week leading up to the meeting, which was to be outdoors in a baseball field, a local partner completely backed out of support. (They had pledged a small stage and sound system.) They told me that they didn't think it was wise to do the meeting at the location I chose and during the time period I chose because of the ongoing issues with the pandemic and how it might look to some of their leadership and partners if they were to partner with me.

I'm all for safety, but statistics showed the virus had a 99.97 percent survival rate, much like that of the flu. I was totally blindsided, shocked, and now scrambling. On top of that, the weather was showing wind and snow with freezing temperatures during the meeting. Some close friends bought me a portable speaker, and on the day of the event, I went and stood on the pitcher's mound on a freezing cold, snowy Tacoma day, and preached to a small group of about fifteen people. I came to find out that only one of them came after seeing the ads. She had just seen the flyer a few hours beforehand and drove over. Praise God, she heard the gospel that day.

After all was said and done, I drove home wrestling with what could be seen in worldly or even ministry standards as a failure. I felt nothing but opposition on all sides, and what was supposed to be a rally-style event and a catalyst for future events all leading up to the nationwide tour felt like a dud. I felt like the message I preached was off because I had one message in mind, but most of the people who showed up were my friends, so I felt strange preaching the gospel to them (they were already burning for Jesus), which resulted in a shoot-from-the-hip message in horrid weather.

Can you picture it? I laugh to myself now as I look back. I see the faith that God was building within me. I also see the obedience, which honestly probably came from stubbornness as well. Even though the event itself seemed like a failure, I knew that God honored my yes and that a little bit more fear of man was broken off me. I've learned in my seven years of walking with God that any chance I get to break off fear of man, I do it. I cannot afford to be driven by the opinions of creations when I have the attention of the Creator.

The rest of the winter and into the spring were filled with evangelistic gatherings around Pierce and King County, as well as making content for social media and preparing for the upcoming summer tour. By the time April 2021 rolled around, the summer tour was nearly fully funded by my social media followers' donations. I couldn't believe that I could raise forty thousand dollars in just over six months. I was posting flyers and graphics for each city, making videos, calling locals in each one to assemble, and booking flights, hotels, and rental cars. It was a ton of work. But God had called me to do this, and I was getting excited at the idea of traveling my country and preaching the gospel in major cities to people that I'd never met.

I had saved up a lot of time off for the summer so that I could take a week off work to preach, then come back for a few days, then leave again, and so on. Everything in the plan was beginning to make sense until the day that Jessica and I found out that we were pregnant. All of a sudden, I was wondering how I was going to do the tour and leave Jessica for days or even a week at a time while she was pregnant. I was also beginning to think about the fact that I was burning all my time off to do this crusade during the summer, but Jessica was due in November, which meant I would have no days off and would have to take leave without pay. Could we sustain ourselves for a month or two with no income and a new baby? All these thoughts came to my mind. As we began to make plans to save up and prepare for no income for a few months, the Lord opened the doors to ministry, and we moved to Texas.

That season was trying for our faith, but the whole way, I am proud to say that we trusted in God. That doesn't mean that every day, we woke up, feeling like we were on fire with bulletproof vests on. What it means is that every day, whether feeling amazing or weak, whether full of faith or full of doubt, we *chose* to trust in God. We made the decision, despite all opposition, all adversity, all evidence that would cause us to doubt, to trust God. *That* is how you win in the fight of faith.

As you read about this season that Jess and I walked through, I'm sure that it provoked some thoughts about your own trials. I'd love for you to examine your life right now and see how God has sustained you through the hardest and most difficult seasons. Look back on the times that it felt like He wasn't speaking and see how He intentionally kept quiet to see what you would do. God doesn't speak because He isn't there; He stays quiet when He knows that He's already put everything inside you that you need to endure, and He's believing that you'll overcome by living by faith and not by the flesh. Take some time to thank God for how He's brought you through each season and gotten you to where you're at right now. Even if you don't prefer to remain in the place you are right now, know that just like the weather, seasons change, but God remains the same.

2021 US Gospel Crusade

June arrived, and the gospel crusade was set to begin. Jessica and I had been in Texas for around a month and were beginning to get our bearings when the time for me to leave arrived. My first stop was Tacoma. I had chosen this purposely because while planning, I lived there and started in my own town and made my way down the coast. Now that I lived in Texas, I was flying back to my old city to preach.

Jessica assured me that she would be fine and encouraged me every step of the way to do what God had called me to do. We had a great group of friends who were nearby if Jess needed anything, even just some company. With that in mind, I left for the first leg of the tour. I traveled and preached for five days in a row, from Tacoma down to San Diego. Each night, I saw salvations, physical and emotional healings, and deliverances from demons. The meetings ranged in size from forty in Tacoma, to five in Sacramento, to nearly one hundred in San Diego on the beach. God moved powerfully, and my faith was rapidly rising. Little did I know that back home, my wife was undergoing intense spiritual warfare as she heard lies that she would die during labor and never meet our son.

As the weeks went by and the tour progressed, I was so thankful to be a full-time preacher. God blessed us greatly, and it became so evident by the fact that I was able to be home and with my family in between each leg of the tour. The original plan was to travel and preach, then fly back to Tacoma and work a week at my job, then fly back out and repeat. After traveling and preaching for a week at a time, I was exhausted from ministering for more than three hours each night and traveling for four to five hours each morning. On top of that, I would've hardly ever seen Jessica during that summer between the tour and work. God knew our situation and made a way where there seemed no way. Even knowing things would be difficult, we desired His presence and followed His voice, saying yes when it looked hard.

We had no idea that we'd be in Texas, enjoying so much time together between stops, but God did. I'm thankful that we said yes to Him before knowing any of this. Things like that show you that your love for God and desire to be obedient are genuine. It would've sounded like a dream to know that I'd be in full-time ministry in Texas. (No offense to Washington, but Texas living is a dream.) That would have been so easy to say yes to. But knowing that we gave God our plans when it wasn't easy and wasn't beautiful shows that we were willing to do whatever it took to follow Him. That isn't because we are awesome or super anointed but because we were desperate for Him and have known Him long enough to know that life apart from obedience is no life at all.

This is a great time to reflect on the decisions or even indecisions you've made. Are you giving God your yes when it's tough, or if you're being totally honest with yourself, do you need to know everything and see that it looks pretty easy before you do? I hope you are provoked to give God your everything in the midst of confusion and uncertainty. He is more than worthy of all we could give. I urge you not to wait for things to look perfect and feel comfortable to follow God. First, that's not true obedience. That's waiting for things to be good for your own benefit, which is actually selfish in nature. But second, the perfect, comfortable time to follow God, with all your questions answered and with no adversity, will probably never come. You'll find yourself old and gray, still waiting on that opportunity to follow God when it feels right. Don't let time pass while you decide whether or not to give God everything. The time is now!

One night marked our family forever, what the enemy meant for bad but God redeemed for our good and His glory. It was August 21, 2021, and my birthday was the next day. Jessica and I had been hanging out, watching a show, and eating one of my favorite homemade desserts called ooey-gooey butter bars. It's basically made with cream cheese and powdered sugar, and like the name says, every bite is ooey-gooey-buttery deliciousness. The recipe is from a family friend, and I've loved it since I was a young boy. Anyway, I was sitting and eating those and talking to Jessica as I prepared to go to TopGolf with a few friends later.

All of a sudden, I felt that same feeling as we did in our room when the enemy walked in and threw Jess into a seizure. The next thing I knew, she began convulsing on the couch. I began to pray, and shortly after it started, she came out of it. I will say that each time, the seizures were relatively short, and each time she recovered faster than the previous one, but I still hated that they happened. This time, however, was different because she was seven months pregnant with Elijah. I was determined to not let fear wreak havoc on my mind, and Jessica and I prayed together that night in faith that God would redeem what had happened

I was scheduled to leave on another leg of the tour on August 23, just two days later, and Jessica felt from God that I was still supposed to go. When praying, I felt like God spoke to me. "What's changed? What about the seizure changes anything I've called you to do?" We actually sat down and thought about what I believed I heard from God, and neither one of us could figure out anything that had changed. We set it in our hearts and minds to live as if it had never happened. We refused to dwell on it or let the enemy make it into a big thing.

Naturally, though, we had to navigate practical matters. Jess and I were planning a home birth with a midwife, so we called her to let her know what happened. She told us that unfortunately, she would be unable to work with us unless we saw a neurologist and got Jessica on medication because she was now considered high risk. Jessica still felt the same resolve as previously that she was never to return to medication.

I need to make something clear here. This is something she believes she heard from God and was walking out in faith. It would be foolishness for you to hear this, and without prayer or hearing from God in your own relationship to try to apply what Jessica was walking through to your own life. It would be foolish to read this and immediately go dump all your medication down the drain. Jessica and I were walking under intense conviction from God, knowing that on the other side of our faith was either life or death. We were willing to take that risk in our pursuit of obedience to Him. Do not use other people's testimonies or faith as a plug and play for your own life. Walk in relationship with God, commune with Him, and navigate your life *with Him.* Be led by Him, not me. You can absolutely be inspired and provoked by our testimony, but don't try to apply these principles as a blanket rule to your own life. Without wisdom, you could make a foolish and costly mistake.

Because Jessica and I refused to get on medication or even go talk to a neurologist (we saw no need), we terminated care with our midwife. Jess was seven months pregnant. After this radical step of faith, Jess told me that she was prepared in her heart to have an unassisted birth with just the two of us. As scary as that sounded, I saw no other option for the insane faith journey we had found ourselves on. It was not that we were afraid or too prideful to have a hospital birth or get help. If you read our story that way, you're reading it with the wrong perspective. Jessica and I had a *conviction.* To us, disobeying our conviction felt like sin, and we'd rather die than sin. Call us radical, but we just wanted to hear God and then boldly follow what He said.

We called some of our best friends, Jonah and Alexis Coyne, to pray for us, and during the conversation we asked if Alexis, who served as a doula, would consider doing the birth for us when the time came. She agreed, we all prayed, and Jessica and I were immediately filled with faith, hope, and excitement.

I finished out the tour, seeing more and more souls come to Jesus and insane physical healings, including a wheelchair-bound teenaged girl instantly healed. She danced away from the meeting and later had the miracle medically confirmed, as every trace of her disorder was indiscoverable by doctors. In Miami, we saw more than two hundred people gather and even more in New York City. (That meeting was held as a tropical storm smashed into the city that night.)

After this tour, opportunities to preach began to open up. My social media was taking off, and I was nearing one million followers on TikTok and one hundred thousand on Instagram. I also had over one hundred thousand subscribers on YouTube. God was blowing up every aspect of the ministry, and Jessica and I felt as if we were turning a corner. We felt like a new thing was happening. Around that time, an organization called Turning Point USA reached out to me and invited me to be a VIP at an annual event they did in Phoenix. Turning Point, of all the names! Ha! Jessica and I laughed as we knew the Lord was speaking very clearly to us.

A few months after the tour ended, on Thanksgiving Day 2021, my son, Elijah, was born at home in our bedroom with only me and Alexis present. Laughing, my wife pushed out our son naturally with no anesthesia. No, literally, she was laughing while pushing out his head! I'm here to tell you that God works in the most incredible ways. The months and months we spent contending for a supernatural birth came to fruition that day. Jessica gave birth to our son under a sign hanging on our wall that says "I have seen the goodness of God." We truly had seen His goodness, and all we could do was celebrate and cry tears of joy and thankfulness.

Your Next Leap of Faith

This chapter was packed with major leaps of faith, more than I'd expected to face in a single year, let alone in six months. If I've learned anything as a Christian, it's that following God is a scary, amazing, humbling roller-coaster ride—a ride that will always end in His glory and for our good—but the journey is filled with unknowns, giants to overcome, and fears to tear down. I always wonder as I write stories like this what people are thinking. Sometimes I read what I've written or reflect on what God has brought me through, and I can hardly believe it myself, and I've lived it. I quickly learn not only to trust God but also to remove any limitations or boxes I've put on Him.

I've been in situations I'd never imagined I'd be in, stood before people I never thought I'd stand before, and done things I'd never thought I'd do (like catching my newborn son during a home birth on the floor of my bedroom). As you read my experiences, reflect on your walk with Jesus and even your outlook and perspective on life in general. What boxes have you put on God? What limitations have you put on His limitless power, maybe without even knowing or meaning to? Right now, I want to challenge you to pray a dangerous prayer.

God, lead me into the deep. Lead me into the unknown. I want to know your mysteries. I want to see you move in ways I could never experience by living comfortably. Wreck life plans of my own making and make them your own.

Your next leap of faith could be one act of obedience away. Practically, I find it helpful to write down what God is speaking. Take the next few moments after we pause and pray and write down at least one thing or as many as God puts on your heart that you feel God is asking you to step into or steward differently or better. Maybe God has asked you to start a Bible study or a house church or a small group or a live stream. Maybe He's asked you to disciple someone. Whatever it is, your next leap of faith can't happen if you remain standing still. Watch what God will do when you begin to move your feet in faith. You can do this.

Pause and Pray

Father, I thank you in the name of Jesus for how you're working in my life. I praise you for being my guide, my leader, my master, and my Savior. I honor you for being faithful, amazing, and awesome in power. I ask you right now to make much of my faith in you. Take my small yes and do something incredible with it for your glory. I want to know you more. I want to give you all the honor that you deserve. I want to praise you with my life and by my obedience. Today, I'm asking you to provoke me in any areas that have become comfortable or stagnant. Help me to grow, Lord. If there is any unbelief in my life that is limiting me from giving you everything, expose it and uproot it. I want to burn for you! Help me stay on fire and never let me go out. I love you, God, and I pray all of this in Jesus's name. Amen.

9

Walking in Freedom and Entering Rest

When all you're accustomed to is war, how do you handle life when it's time to rest? When I was in the military, it was hard to do this. Even after coming home from my deployment to Afghanistan, I was ready to go back within a few days. I felt out of place at home, misunderstood, and almost in this place of fear like I was missing out on what was happening back there. Those who are veterans and have served in war know what I'm talking about. But for those who haven't served, maybe you can relate to this comparison.

Think about being on a team and getting subbed out of the game. Your team is still playing, and yes, you may need to rest, but you long to be back in it so that you can help your teammates out and be a part of the effort. In some strange and even unhealthy way, this is how I felt when the warring in my life stopped. Fast-forward to a few months after Elijah was born. The tour was over, and Jessica and I were settling into parent life. I realized that I had forgotten how to rest.

The Bible doesn't tell us to strive for many things, but one of the things we are told to do regarding rest is to labor to enter into it. Hebrews 4 is an excellent chapter on rest, and verse 11 says, "Let us therefore be diligent to enter that rest." In this chapter, the Bible even speaks of God resting from all that He had done. If God rested, surely we ought to as well.

However, it isn't that easy when you're used to working, warring, and constantly *doing*. I always found it interesting that in all of our working, we are told to actually work to enter rest. It isn't always easy to just rest. Resting is more than just sitting on a couch with an empty calendar. Resting is trusting. Resting is believing. Resting is yielding to God. It's believing that He is enough to sustain, fulfill, and accomplish everything He intends to. An inability to rest actually might be rooted in a place of unbelief or fear; fear that if you don't do enough, God will be displeased or won't continue to provide.

This way of thinking can quickly turn from an innocent lack of understanding to a demonic slave driver, working you to the bone and never letting up. But I didn't know how to function in a season of rest. God had delivered us from all the trials we were facing in that season, and now we were in a new season without war. Finances were secure, Jessica's health was consistently doing well, I was traveling and preaching, and life was good. Even in this goodness, I felt off, and dare I say, uncomfortable.

If I had to describe how I felt, it seemed as if I was constantly waiting for something bad to happen, for the other shoe to drop. Jessica and I had been regularly warring in prayer in our bedroom or throughout our home. I had gotten so used to trials and fires coming against us that when the pressure finally let up, I didn't know what to do with myself. Anxiety began to creep in because I started to believe the lie that you couldn't just live your life in peace; something always had to be wrong.

Have you ever dealt with this? I'm talking about walking through this recently for myself. I'm writing this in November 2022, and I just navigated this in January 2022. God had to show me how to rest. I think it's easy when you're warring all the time because you get into this zone. For Jess and me, the days would be pretty good, and then everything with her health would seem to take a dive at or around dinnertime. It wasn't that we expected this to happen or welcomed it by any means, but many of you know that when something becomes somewhat of a routine, you start to brace for it.

Each day, we'd go about our normal activities, waking up early to be with Jesus. I'd go play golf or hit a bucket of balls from 6:30 to 7:30 a.m., then come home for breakfast with the family, and then start my workday. After lunch, I'd make some content for social media, and Jess and I would hang out with Elijah. Right around dinner, we would almost prepare ourselves for the spiritual battle that was coming. We'd go up into our room and lie on the floor, or I'd lie on the floor while Jess was in the bed, and we'd pray, sometimes for hours. Prayer and worship and talking lasted until around nine o'clock at night, and then we'd try to get some sleep.

Some days and weeks, this felt like it was our normal. When you're in a season like that, as hard as it is to go through, it's also almost easy in a sense. You don't have to do much thinking because your mind is preoccupied with the battle you're facing. You're so focused on staying in the presence of God and contending for breakthrough that other issues of life that usually try to rule the day seem nonexistent. Life becomes simple when only one or two things occupy your mind.

This was true in Afghanistan as well. As hard or as challenging as war was, there is a simplicity to the lifestyle over there that you can only find in that environment. In regard to spiritual warfare, there is also a closeness you find with Jesus that you cannot experience in peacetime. Not that Jesus isn't always close, but it's a different kind of closeness during a trial, and many of you know what I mean. Jess has even gone as far as to say that it's hard for her to not miss the nearness of Jesus in the hardest seasons of our life.

The difference when you're in a time of peace and not actively warring for something is that you can find a new routine. From my experience, if you are not diligent about spending time with the Lord, you can easily find a comfortable routine that forsakes time and intimacy with Him. I've found that a lie swirls around Christians when life is good, and this subconscious lie is driving many away from going deeper with God and living a life of consistent intimacy. People do not intentionally believe this lie: Things are good, and you don't *need* God right now.

Be honest with me, when you're in a trial and life is coming at you hard, how aware do you become of your need for God? My answer is, extremely aware. I've wept on my bedroom floor because I needed Him so badly. Are you ready for the lie? The lie is that when the war stops and life is great and wonderful, money is coming in, and everyone's health is good, then I don't need God just as much as I did on that bedroom floor. Have you ever believed that lie? I'm willing to bet your answer is yes, because I believe we all struggle with this as Christians. Why do we struggle with it? Because we are not aware of our need for God at *all* times.

Only the believer who sees their unchanging desperation for God will be unshaken by the seasons. If your need for God is seasonal, you'll find your faith will be too. If your need for God is circumstantial, you'll find that your peace is too. If your need for God is recognized only in the trials, then your joy will only come in their absence. This roller coaster of sensual living is demonic and prevents countless believers from walking in harmony. The mature believer will recognize their need for God is just as great on their best day as it is on their worst. Do you want a piece of advice that will keep you sober-minded and constantly seeking God in all seasons? Here it is: We never graduate from desperation for Him.

I can't tell you how awful it felt to go to bed one night, and as I turned off the lamp, I thought, *I haven't prayed with Jess in days.* I instantly realized that because life was going well, our time of prayer and intercession had ceased. I told Jessica to get up so that we could pray. It wasn't out of some religious duty or to make sure God was pleased with us. Never! It was from a place of repentance. I experienced godly sorrow for allowing the good days we'd had to take over my awareness of my constant need for Jesus. We both confessed that we'd been distracted by the blessings of God and forgotten the need. We repented and began to worship and praise God and thank Him for all that He'd done. We vowed to each other to stay diligent about prayer; whether crying out to God during the tough seasons or worshiping Him when the answers came, we were not going to miss that time together anymore. You don't need God more when the trial comes, and you don't need Him less when things are good. You need Him always.

Crushing the Orphan Spirit

As I dove into my fear of this season of joy and peace and rest, I desired to find the root of it all. Yes, it's absolutely rooted in control and anxiety, a negative perspective of the future. But deeper than control is the inability to receive. I find that this issue plagues many believers and reveals that we don't fully understand what it means to be born again. Our inability to receive from God shows that we still don't comprehend His feelings toward us and what He paid for on the cross through His Son.

Jesus didn't die to get us into heaven. He didn't die because we were sinners. The Bible says that He died *while* we were yet sinners (Romans 5:8), but that doesn't reveal His motivation. The motivation for Jesus going to the cross was to restore lost sons and daughters to the Father. Think about this: The Bible says that Jesus came "to save that which was lost" (Matthew 18:11). What was lost? It wasn't heaven—it was relationship. Jesus came to crush the orphan spirit and give us the Spirit of the One True God.

He came to deliver us from sin and from self. Why self? Because preservation of self and pride was the first sign of sin in the garden. When God was walking through the garden in the cool of the day (Genesis 3:8), Adam and Eve hid. When God asked them if they disobeyed, Adam responded, "It was the woman you gave me." Adam immediately shifted the blame to Eve to try to preserve himself. The first sign of sin was the inability to take accountability for his own actions and to attempt to save face by making someone else take the blame. People still do it today, and this is why Jesus said if we want to come after Him, the first thing we have to do is deny ourselves (Luke 9:23).

Since Jesus paid the price on the cross for us to be forgiven and cleansed of sin, that selfish nature can be removed as the old self is put to death, and that heart of stone is replaced with a heart of flesh. We are made into new creations and now have hearts for God and for others. Yes, we work out our salvation daily, but we are working on dying to self and living for Christ. The world cannot die to themselves because they are completely alive for self. Apart from Christ, there is no true incentive to die to self. Dying to self in the world's terms will put you behind and beneath, but in the kingdom of God, this is exactly how to be exalted. Jesus said that "the last will be first, and the first last" (Matthew 20:16).

All this points to a humbling that happens when we come to the cross and a daily humbling that must take place in order for us to not become prideful. Pride will cause you to reject God's love. Did you know that the inability to be forgiven is pride? It's saying, "You don't know what I've done. I've done too much. I can't be forgiven." The Bible says that the blood of Jesus is strong enough to take on the sins of the whole world and cleanse them. Even the worst sinner in history can be forgiven by the power of the blood of Jesus. Just one drop will do the job. For any human to say that they can't be forgiven by God would be to say that your particular sins are too much and that Jesus's blood is no match for them. It takes humility to come to Christ and say, "Jesus, I have sinned. I believe you can forgive me, and I receive that forgiveness in my life. I will follow you. Thank you for making me brand new. I believe that you don't hold my sin against me." It takes humility to walk in forgiveness.

It also takes humility to rest. Pride says, "I know that God rested on the seventh day, but I need to work." You are certainly not above God. If He rested, you too must rest. You must humble yourself to receive His rest. You must strive to enter into His rest. This humble submission is what an obedient son or daughter does when they crawl up into the lap of their mom or dad. It takes humility to place yourself in the lap or arms of a parent. The Bible says that "God resists the proud" (James 4:6), and the opposite is true as well. It is pride to resist God.

An orphan has no parent and must fend for themselves. An orphan cannot rest, but a child with a Father can. In this season, I was forced to admit to God and to myself that in some areas, I had taken on an orphan spirit. As soon as God made me aware of this, I confessed it to Him and repented of not receiving everything He had for me. I told Him how I longed to trust Him. It was easy to trust Him to carry me through trials and to have faith that we would overcome, but when life was great, I found myself becoming scared of the next trial, not knowing when it would come, what it would look like, or how severe it would be. God showed me that I was allowing demonic strongholds (wrong ways of thinking) to occupy my mind. I tore them down with the truth of His Word and immediately began to walk in freedom.

The amazing part about truth is that it will set you free instantly. Sure, you must take some practical steps in order to see a full manifestation of that freedom. As you can imagine, while my ways of thinking were being corrected, I still had the temptations to doubt and fear. However, when those came, I recognized them instantly and began to take them captive and make them obedient to Christ. I was warring again, but this time to maintain the peace that I had already been given.

Many people think that they need to say a prayer to receive peace, but the Bible says that Jesus has already given it to us. What we actually need to do is fight to stay aware of it. We must fight to not let the enemy rob us of our peace and joy. Someone can't rob what you don't own. God gave you His peace and joy when you were born again, but it is up to you to first, believe it, and second, walk in it.

Taking Thoughts Captive

Whenever you find yourself constantly walking in power, you will be tempted to let pride rise up. As I talked about earlier in the book, I dealt with this early in my walk with Jesus in regard to walking in the miraculous. As I exited a season of warfare, I felt the same familiar spirit try to root itself into my way of thinking, only this time, I saw it coming and dealt with it immediately. That's the amazing thing about wisdom and walking with God. When the enemy tries to come at you with something he's already done before, it feels like an alarm is going off in your spirit.

One day, I was reading something about spiritual warfare on social media. I was interested, so I kept reading, and the post was about not being able to find a spouse. Mind you, Jessica and I had just walked out of a tough few days of interceding for her health, and now I'm reading about someone who's lonely. I could literally *feel* the same things I felt as a new believer, and God spoke to me right away before it could take root.

I told God that I never wanted to look down on someone else or compare my battles with theirs. I'm not better because I've gone through this or that. You're not less than because you didn't. I spoke truth over myself and declared it in my home, that my house would not be a place of comparison. I reminded myself that Christian victory is to have enduring faith, not to win the biggest or most difficult battles. I also reminded myself that my brothers and sisters in Christ are there for me to pour into and encourage, receive from, and celebrate with. We are not in a competition.

I'm so thankful for the voice of the Lord exposing the plans of the enemy and even any fleshly thoughts that tried to rise up. Comparison is a killer, and it also is a breeding ground for pride. Kill comparison and kill your pride before they kill you.

Taking these thoughts captive is actually easy to do; it's staying consistent that can be the challenge. I know that when I'm in a trial or even just exhausted from a long or challenging day, my will to fight is weak. But I know that the Bible says to take *every* thought captive. Every single one! I like to compare it to doing the dishes after cooking. I am a big fan of cooking, especially steaks. I know that after dinner, if I don't clean the pan right away, the oil and the seasoning will harden and be especially difficult to remove later. If I leave it overnight without washing it, it's going to be a nightmare to get off.

This is how intrusive and negative thoughts work too. The longer you let a thought sit in your mind, unchecked and undealt with, the more stuck it will become. After long enough, it will harden and require more work to get off than if you had just dealt with it in the first place despite your fatigue or lack of desire to do so. For those really-hard-to-clean pans, you might have to soak them for a couple of hours or even overnight. The same is true with our minds. The longer you've allowed something to sit in your mind, the longer you'll need to soak in

God's presence and truth for it to be uprooted. The good news is that the answer to deliverance is always the truth of God's Word.

Maybe you're reading this, and you're nodding your head like, "Wow, this is exactly what I deal with." I want to give you a tip on how to take thoughts captive that will change your life. I learned this when I was a new believer, and to this day, it still works because it's biblical.

We often hear about taking thoughts captive, but many people that I meet and preach to don't actually know how to do it. Most of the church at large tends to believe that taking thoughts captive means rebuking and binding. "Satan, I rebuke you in Jesus's name! Evil spirits, I bind you and command you to leave. Get thee behind me, Satan!"

Many faithful prayer warriors do this, but sadly, many people still struggle with intrusive thoughts, and they're too burned out to deal with them. This leads to discouragement, apathy, and, for some, even to walking away from their faith. I believe we are burned out because we've spent all of that time rebuking and binding but have no revelation of truth. We end up finishing a prayer session with no answers, no deliverance, and a heightened awareness of our issues. Think about it, if you spend thirty minutes praying, and all you're doing is rebuking, at the end of that thirty minutes, you'll be very aware of your issues but won't have any solutions. The Bible says we are destroyed by what we don't know. So let's get some knowledge.

The thing that destroys a lie is truth. Truth instantly deflates a lie and makes it powerless. When the enemy speaks to you, you may indeed need to bind and rebuke—that's biblical. But when the enemy is lying to you, you can easily defeat him by speaking what's true. You don't need to bind a lie—you need to elevate truth. This is why the Bible says to take captive what exalts itself above the knowledge of Christ. The lies of the enemy are thrown at you in order to try to put a ceiling over your life and a barrier between you and God.

Romans 8:38–39 says that nothing can separate you from the love of God. The enemy might tell you that God's mad at you, but it isn't true. The enemy might try to make you *feel* like you're worthless, but it isn't true. The enemy might tell you that you'll never be forgiven, but it isn't true. The enemy might even tell you that you should end your own life, but that isn't true. These lies don't need to be bound; they need to be destroyed with truth. Truth always wins over a lie. This is why the Bible says wherever the Spirit of the Lord is, there is freedom (2 Corinthians 3:17). The Bible says that the Spirit of the Lord will lead you into all truth (John 16:13). So wherever truth is, there is freedom.

Here's a practical example of how to take a thought captive. One day, I was driving in my Mustang GT. Back when I was a young lieutenant in the army, I loved cruising around in that thing. It was the first car that I bought myself when I was twenty. I had it race-tuned and set up with straight pipes, cold air intake, long tube headers, and Flowmasters on the back. That car was awesome. For you non-car people who didn't understand any of that, just picture a really cool-looking Matchbox car that sounded mean and was fast.

One beautiful day in the Pacific Northwest, I was driving down the highway and randomly thought: *You should drive your car off the road into that wall and kill yourself.* Now, if I had a wrong view of myself or of God, I might think that I had a demon inside me. I might've texted a few friends for prayer and asked them to come deliver me because I was having suicidal thoughts. I might've gotten afraid and anxious and cried out to God and asked Him why this was happening to me, because I thought I was born again.

However, I knew my identity in Christ. I knew that God lived inside me and possessed me. I could not be possessed by a demon because I'm owned by God. I was bought with a price. I knew those thoughts didn't come from inside of me because I rejected and hated those thoughts. They literally felt like an intruder had come in and planted them in my mind. I instantly began to pray and said something like this. *"Father, I thank you in the name of Jesus for my life. Thank you, God, that I have no desire to end my life. I love you so much, and I love this life that you've blessed me with. I desire to follow you all of my days, and I thank you that by your Spirit, you've shown me that this is not my thought, and I disagree with it completely. Thanks for loving me, God. In Jesus's name. Amen."* That was it. (This is exactly how you take thoughts captive.) Just like that, the thought was crushed, and I actually was in a great mood because I'd just encouraged myself in the truth of God and spent some time talking with Him. No rebuking, no binding, just speaking truth.

Let's look at another example just so that you can really get this way of praying and thinking rooted in your mind. Have you ever had a random thought from your past come to mind, and it made you feel dirty? Maybe something you've done or a situation you've been in, or an old habit or addiction that flies across the screen of your mind. The last thing you need in that moment is to call out for prayer and deliverance. These are thoughts or suggestions from the enemy. The enemy is trying to see if he can own you again, but you already know that you're not up for sale. Instead of graying out and feeling condemned and dirty and eventually backsliding, this is how you deal with that: *Father, I thank you right now in the name of Jesus for making me so pure. Thank you, God, for loving me so much that you saved me from who I was and made me someone brand-new. Thank you, God, that when these thoughts come to my mind, I absolutely hate them and want nothing to do with them because you've made me so clean. There was a day when these thoughts might've sent me spiraling or even a time when I would've entertained them, but now I know I've been washed by the blood and my desire is righteousness. Thank you for illuminating my spirit and shining your light inside me. I love you, God, and I want to serve, love, and follow you all of my days. In Jesus's name. Amen.*

That kind of prayer will increase your intimacy with God, keep your mind fixed on Him at all times, and pull the rug out from under the plans of the enemy. The enemy knows that for most Christians, those sensual suggestions will send them running and get them feeling

Your Next Leap of Faith

We've covered a lot on spiritual warfare, resting, pride, and taking thoughts captive. These few things, if stewarded well, can keep you burning for Jesus and unfazed by the enemy. Your next leap of faith is going to be internal. For some of you, the warfare and thoughts can get so intense that you lose your will to fight because you are overwhelmed. I want to help stoke that fire within you to fight.

The first thing I want you to do is to write down a number from 0 to 100 percent in a notebook. This number is the percentage of thoughts you think you take captive every day.

The next thing I want you to do is rate on a scale of 1 to 10 how badly you are affected by intrusive or negative thoughts. Ten would be considered debilitating, and one would be virtually unaffected. From what I have seen, most people who take a lower percentage of thoughts captive are the most affected by them. This is because more thoughts are being allowed to fester and sit in your mind. Writing these numbers down can give you a good idea of how diligent (or not) you are. I want you to then make a point to drive that first number up. I'd love to see you living a life where you're taking 100 percent of the negative thoughts captive.

Even if it's a ten-second prayer, this next week, I want to challenge you to not let any negative thoughts sit in your mind. Take them all captive, and pray in the way I taught in this chapter. Since this is scriptural and not my good idea, I can guarantee you that you will have a more peaceful, joyful week. You may be dealing with lies and accusations, but you'll take them to the Father and be encouraged by truth. If you want to move forward in your life on this journey of faith, you can't be bogged down by lies.

Pause and Pray

Father, thank you in Jesus's name for the power over the enemy. Thank you for equipping me to win every spiritual battle, because you, Jesus, have already overcome. Thank you, God, that I will overcome as long as I continue to trust in you. Right now, I command every demonic spirit bringing intrusive thoughts into my life to leave in the name of Jesus. I thank you, Lord, that every assignment of intrusive thoughts and lies will be canceled in Jesus's name. I love you and thank you for always being with me. I am never alone. I pray these things in your name. Amen.

10

Leaning on God's Grace and Learning to Endure

After a year of being with One Voice Student Missions, I felt a pull from God to branch off and begin my own organization. My heart was (and is) burning for the discipleship of young adults, the equipping of millennials, and empowering of the baby boomers. I desire to see all generations being used by God in their full capacity. Traveling and preaching will continue to be my focus, but I'm not writing the curriculum for a School of Kingdom Living. I was changed forever through Dan Mohler's School of Kingdom Living; however, it was only held once. Thankfully, the videos are available on YouTube, which are just as powerful.

I thought, *What if I begin holding schools every few months?* There is something about in-person learning that you can't receive over a video screen. We have so many digital options now: social media, Zoom, Face-Time, live-streaming church, and more. I am pushing more than ever for in-person gatherings, face-to-face discipleship and fellowship, and that's what this school will be. I started a nonprofit called Overcomers Inc. in Texas and am in the early stages of development, but I have an excitement that I've never felt before! You can follow @overcomer_ministries on Instagram to keep up with what is happening, but as always, all updates for what I'm doing can be found on my personal page @shane.winnings.

With all of this, there is a temptation to compare with other ministries. Regardless of how close you are with the Lord, temptation will never go away. Even Jesus was tempted, and He was closer to God than anyone. The key is to maintain a Christlike perspective. Ministries are, hopefully, all out for the same reason: to win souls and help them walk with Jesus every day of their lives.

We are not competitors. The key to staying humble and in a place of trust in seasons like this, especially when you're building something new, is to lean on God's grace. When you're creating a new thing, it's easy to look around you at what everyone else is doing and wish you were further along, more connected, more established, better funded, fully staffed, and the list goes on. The practical side to this is looking at what successful organizations are doing and mirroring some of their practices, but any comparison (or maybe "analytical observations" is a better term) that doesn't inspire you is unhealthy. If, as you look out, you feel discouraged or insignificant, you can be sure that you're listening to the wrong voice.

God's grace will carry you through the trials, the good days, and the in-between times. The following verse always encourages me to remember that God is sovereign, He sees all things and won't let life crush me to the point of completely breaking.

> No temptation has overtaken you except such as is common to man; but God is faithful, who will not allow you to be tempted beyond what you are able, but with the temptation will also make the way of escape, that you may be able to bear it.
>
> 1 Corinthians 10:13

At times, it can feel (there's that word again) as if God isn't present. But as we've discussed and as the Bible teaches, our feelings are horrible leaders. This verse gives me strength when I'm feeling tempted to doubt God's presence in my life. I encourage myself in the Word, and God is always faithful to keep His Word. Grace is getting a gift you don't deserve. The grace of God brought salvation to the world. The grace of God sent His Son, Jesus, to the cross. The grace of God extended forgiveness to a world that was cut off from Him because of sin. By God's grace in your life, He holds nothing against you when you become born again. Isn't that amazing? He gives you the gift of salvation, which includes forgiveness and forgetting all sins. He gives you a brand-new heart and a new mind. God is gracious.

Maybe today as you read this, you find it hard to connect with God's grace. People sometimes see what's going on in the world and allow the issues of the day to matter more than what matters most. They sometimes let what the enemy is saying speak louder that what God has already spoken.

Let us do what David does in the Psalms. He cries and complains like the rest of us, but he never ends a passage there. He always encourages himself in the Lord. He always establishes who God is in the midst of his pain and suffering. He always worships and glorifies the Lord because of His faithfulness.

If you're struggling to connect with the grace, mercy, or love of God today, begin to declare it in the midst of your struggle. You can pray the following: *God, help my unbelief. Help me right now to see you rightly. I declare your goodness over my life, even when I can't see it. I believe that you're working things out for my good, even when everything around me feels like you're not. I choose to believe that you're faithful, even when I can't hear you speaking.*

By doing this, you're actually releasing faith, regardless of what you feel. Faith is believing in what you can't see. It takes real faith to declare the promises and nature of God in the face of doubt. When it hurts and you still worship, you show the enemy that you really do believe. Anyone can worship God when things are great. Anyone can call God faithful when they are walking in the fulfillment of His promises. What about when you aren't seeing results? What about when He's silent? Will you still praise Him?

In the Bible, the devil didn't believe that Job would stay faithful, yet he did. The enemy has the same bet going on today. He doesn't believe that you actually love

God. He thinks that if circumstances change and trials intensify, you'll walk away. Let's make sure to show him that he's wrong. We are God-fearing lovers who aren't alive for a good day but who want to shine for Christ, no matter what.

When we lean on God's grace daily, we wake up in the awareness that we can accomplish nothing apart from Him. In this humility, we lean on Him even when we feel like we can stand on our own. If I had to give one piece of wisdom to a new believer, it would be that last sentence. When you feel like you're standing, recognize that it's because of Him, and lean again. The Bible says this: "Therefore let him who thinks he stands take heed lest he fall" (1 Corinthians 10:12). When we think we are standing on our own, we open ourselves up to a fall. By leaning on God's grace at all times, we can set ourselves up to flow in His rhythms of grace and walk this life out, fulfilling all the desires He has for us.

Stewardship

In order to walk out God's desires for us, we can't be limited by worldly desires. I pray that my book challenged you to step outside of your routine and your comfort zone and lay it all down for Jesus. I pray that you were inspired by what He's done in my life and the life of my family and have faith to ask God to do it again in yours. These testimonies are not just for me. They show the heart and character of God, and we know that God is unchanging. You don't have to sell all your possessions and move around the country or across the world to follow God. If you don't know what God is saying right now, just do the next right thing.

Often, if I feel like God is being silent, I'll just do whatever is in front of me to the best of my ability. The best way to honor God is to be an excellent steward of what He's given you. The Bible says, "Therefore, whether you eat or drink, or whatever you do, do all to the glory of God" (1 Corinthians 10:31). No matter what we're doing, even something that seems so insignificant like eating or drinking, we are called to do it to the glory of God.

What are some things in your life that you can be stewarding better? Sometimes we spread ourselves so thin that we do a handful of things above average instead of a few excellently. Are you trying to steward too much? Maybe it's time to reevaluate where your priorities are and ask God if you're supposed to be carrying everything that you are.

I can get like that at times. I'll start a project, then a few weeks later I'll get another idea, and then another. Before long, I've worked so hard on the new thing that the old thing has taken a back seat. Then, I'll feel bad for letting that slip and try to get it going again, but the cycle repeats itself. It took me nearly a year to really sit down and figure out what I could handle. I then began to pray and present these things to God and ask Him for guidance. As a result, I trimmed back a few obligations and stepped others up. I now feel like I'm in the best place of my life. I am running a few different things but in a manner that I believe brings glory to God.

There is a story in the Bible about stewardship, where three different people are given different amounts of coins. (See Matthew 25:14–30.) One hid their money while the other two traded and ended up doubling theirs. When the master returned, he was pleased with those who went and did something with their coins but was furious with the one who hid his in the ground. When asked why he hid it, he responded that he was afraid of losing it. The master responded by calling that servant "lazy and wicked" (Matthew 10:26).

There is a principle here for us. When God gives you something, He's not looking for you to keep it to yourself and live timidly. God is looking for you to take a leap of faith. The other two servants who doubled their money did so because they went out and worked. It required effort, and the master was pleased.

Would God be pleased with your effort with what He's given you? Have you stewarded the gifts, talents, time, and treasure that He's put in your hand? In that parable, Jesus said that because they were faithful over few things, they would be given much. Have you ever found yourself asking for the much without being faithful with the few?

Let's refocus our eyes on Jesus and let our love for Him and His love for us motivate us to live a life in full surrender. When we do this, we will naturally steward everything with excellence because it will be motivated by love, not by works. We aren't God's employees trying to earn His attention or affection. You can't work for a promotion in the kingdom. You aren't trying to make the grade in God's class. You're a son or a daughter who is greatly loved and was paid for by the blood of the most perfect man who ever lived. Let your life be the thank-you.

Your Next Leap of Faith

After completing this book, it's only fitting that you reflect on your life. I'm not necessarily telling you to write your own book, although you might do that. But I want you to do what I've done as I've written this. Writing out all my experiences has boosted my faith in a new and fresh way. There was something so powerful about reviewing my life and retelling every major move of faith or trial that I walked through and declaring how God met me and delivered me in each one.

For your next leap of faith, I'd love to encourage you to take some time over the next week and begin to write or type out some of the highlights of your life, good and bad, and how God provided, sustained, and ultimately delivered you. The best part of this is that even if you are in a trial right now, you'll build faith by reminding yourself of the past victories. You can see the current storm you're in with a perspective that God will do what He's always done. God is faithful! I've learned that when you desperately need faith for the future or the present, look at what God has done in the past. He is the same yesterday, today, and forever. After you do this, I'd love for you to send me a DM on Instagram and tell me what happened in your faith after going back through your life and doing this challenge.

Pause and Pray

As I close this book, let's release faith and declare who God is over our lives, and pray for these words to be carried far and wide to encourage more and more people to go all in for God.

Father, I thank you in the name of Jesus for your great love for me. Thank you for seeing me through every trial I've faced and for being faithful to deliver me from the hand of the enemy. Thank you for setting my feet on solid ground. Lord, I trust in you. I give you my yes today and ask you to make much of it. Make much of yourself in my life, God. I ask you to use my testimony to encourage the lives of others. Give me a heart to share what you've done and not keep it to myself. Thank you that no matter where I find myself in life, you'll always be there with me. I love you, and I praise you for being Lord of my life. In Jesus's name. Amen.

Notes

Chapter 2 Escaping a "But First" Life

1. Yustos Anthony, "But First, by Daniel Kolenda," YouTube, January 6, 2016, 23:40 to 25:30, https://www.youtube.com/watch?v=EOBYlgAqyp0&ab_channel=YustosAnthony.

2. *Merriam-Webster*, s.v. "thankful (*adj.*)," accessed March 1, 2023, https://www.merriam-webster.com/dictionary/thankful.

3. "Express warm approval of," Wordplays.com, accessed March 1, 2023, https://www.wordplays.com/crossword-solver/express-warm-approval-of-(someone%2Fsomething).

Chapter 3 Overcoming Distraction, Deception, and Trauma

1. Wikipedia, s.v., "Lingchi," last modified January 21, 2023, 8:07, https://en.wikipedia.org/wiki/Lingchi.

2. "2022 National Veteran Suicide Prevention Annual Report," Veteran's Administration, September 2022, https://www.mentalhealth.va.gov/docs/data-sheets/2022/2022-National-Veteran-Suicide-Prevention-Annual-Report-FINAL-508.pdf, p. 7.

Chapter 6 Discovering That a Supernatural Life Is Normal Christianity

1. Shane Winnings, "JESUS IS HEALING!! The lord told me to go to the mall . . . ," Facebook, May 19, 2016, https://www.facebook.com/1419143283/videos/10209535367687263/.

Shane Winnings is a former veteran and was deployed to Afghanistan with the US Army Special Forces in 2014. Following his military service, Shane spent five years as a police officer just south of Seattle, working nights in a gang-infested city.

In 2016, God radically encountered Shane. He devoted his life to preaching on the streets and praying for as many people as he could. He left the police force in 2021 to become a traveling preacher and missionary to America. Shane has preached to thousands and seen God move in signs and wonders, but more importantly, in hearts.

Shane is the author of *I Will Always Overcome*, a nine-week devotional that has helped thousands move from lives of fear into faith. Shane is a contributor to Promise Keepers, a long-standing organization with a mission of raising boys into men. He is also a contributor to Turning Point USA Faith, an organization with the desire to see Christian values and principles represented in the educational and political spheres.

Shane is also the CEO and president of Overcomers Inc., a nonprofit with a mission to equip the body of Christ through preaching and teaching, as well as an emphasis on discipling college-aged men. Shane has been married to his wife, Jessica Winnings, for four years, and they are proud parents of Elijah, born Thanksgiving 2021. They reside in McKinney, Texas.